The History of the Pentecostal Movement in North India

Christian Heritage Rediscovered

The Series, as the name suggests, is meant to focus on Christian Faith & Living vis-à-vis topics like Literature & Poetry, Indigenous Philosophizing, Ethical response towards Agriculture, Health & Healing, Science & Technology, Eco-feminist Theology, Sociological approach towards Human Rights, Law & Politics, Arts, History of Ideas, Ancient Civilizations, Cultural Contiguity, Religious Cosmologies & Mysticism, Footsteps of famous Theologians, World Peace & Harmony, Global Capitalism, Network Marketing, Cybertheology, Population & Demographics, Epigraphic Studies, Contextualized Education, and many others. We welcome a Mss. on any topic/s mentioned, whether they are original works, scholarly monographs, collections of conference papers, revised dissertations, or translations of historical documents. Through the Series we, the Publishers, are striving to put forward published works that may help Institutions, Academic Bodies, Researchers, Scholars and the World at large in furthering their respective knowledge and understanding on the concerned subject. We welcome your comments on our efforts and further suggestions on how we can foster the upcoming thought provoking theologically grounded books.

Christian Heritage Rediscovered - 56

The History of the Pentecostal Movement in North India

Unfolding its Social & Theological Contexts

Shaibu Abraham

CWI

Christian World Imprints(TM)

First Published in 2017 by

Christian World Imprints(TM)
Christian Publishing & Books from India
H-12 Bali Nagar, **New Delhi-110015**
info@christianworldimprints.com
www.ChristianWorldImprints.com
Phone: +91 11 25465925

ISBN: 978-93-5148-223-9 (HB) ISBN: 978-93-5148-224-6 (PB)

Cataloging in Publication Data--DK
Courtesy: D.K. Agencies (P) Ltd. <docinfo@dkagencies.com>

Abraham, Shaibu, author.
The history of the Pentecostal movement in North India : unfolding its social & theological contexts / Shaibu Abraham.
pages cm. -- (Christian heritage rediscovered ; 56)
Includes bibliographical references.
ISBN 9789351482239 (HB)
ISBN 9789351482246 (PB)

1. Pentecostalism--India, North--History--20th century. 2. India, North--Church history--20th century. I. Title. II. Series: Christian heritage rediscovered ; 56.

BR1644.5.I4A27 2017 DDC 275.4082 23

Printed in India.

Contents

Dedicated

to

P. M. Mathew

&

Saramma Mathew

My parents who still toil in the North Indian mission field

Preface

The Pentecostal movement is one of the major Christian denominations that is growing fast in India today. The movement attracts people from all castes, classes, languages, people groups and geographical locations. The visible signs of its growth can be seen in urban centers as well as even in interior villages. Some of the largest Christian congregations of India are Pentecostal churches. Anyone who travels in cities and villages of India can see ample evidences of the growth of Pentecostalism among common masses. In South India, the Pentecostal churches are well established and have considerable influence among all the sections of the society. The history, growth and extent of the movement in South India is documented. Theologians, sociologists and religious observers have begun to consider the beliefs and practices of the movement and critically appreciate its social and theological relevance.

In North India, however, the situation is rather different. Pentecostal growth has taken place primarily in rural areas; among the poor, Tribal people, Dalits and lower castes. The Northern Indian States like Rajasthan, Madhya Pradesh, Jharkhand, Chhattisgarh, Punjab, Uttar Pradesh, Haryana, Delhi (incl. NCR), & Uttarakhand (i.e., Uttaranchal) have experienced remarkable growth in Pentecostalism like the other adjoining Indian States - Gujarat, Maharashtra, Orissa, and Bihar. The Pentecostalism is attracting people from Dalits, Tribal-groups and lower castes because its spirituality provides them with a sense of dignity and hope that is non-existent in other sections of Indian society. Most of the people who joined the movement in the beginning were either underprivileged members of the society or people with physical or spiritual troubles. The majority who join Indian Pentecostal churches belong to the younger generation.

The movement had its origin with some of the revival movements in the beginning of the last century which resulted in the growth of Pentecostal churches. Although, the North Indian Pentecostal Movement has grown into considerable extent, its hundred years of history is neither fully documented nor properly analysed. The task of retrieving the history of the North Indian Pentecostal Movement is painstaking as the pioneers of the movement were so engrossed in their mission that they did not bother to write down the history of this vibrant movement. Thus, many of the exciting stories of the movement and its history are lost forever.

Here, effort is made to retrieve the stories of some of the revivals took place in the north and the rapid church growth followed. This work highlights some of the unknown people who became the trailblazers of the movement and the churches that are not part of the established Pentecostal denominations. It also looks into the beginning of the Pentecostal movement in most of the north Indian states and try to bring local histories into prominence. The readers will find some of the stories that are previously unknown but exciting and spiritually edifying. Moreover, a methodology for north Indian Pentecostal history writing is proposed to help the future historians and students of the movement to systematically collect the historical data to present a balanced history of the movement.

Effort has taken to include the history of the most of the mission organisations and church growth movements working in the north Indian states. However, some of them might have been left out because of lack of enough information. It is anticipated that this effort of presenting the history of the north Indian Pentecostal movement will enable some of the researchers to delve deep into the history and theology of the movement and cherish the future generations with a balanced interpretation of the movement.

The history of Pentecostalism in north India is the history of Pentecostal mission and the Church growth movement. It is the encounter of the Gospel with the religio-cultural and socio-political contexts of India. It is the story of the Spirit movement; the bright wind of the Spirit blowing all over the Indian subcontinent; the story of Spirit-filled people who faced the powers of darkness; of their triumphs and failures, joys and sorrows, unity and division, love and hate, their partnerships and even clashes; of divine and human elements working together. As the Pentecostal churches continues to grow in north India, it is vital to reconstruct the lost history of the movement to hand it over to the future generations.

Chapter 1

North Indian Pentecostal History Prospects and Problems

The Pentecostal movement is one of the major Christian denominations in India today. In the Indian sub-continent, the Pentecostal movement is growing fast. According to the *World Christian Encyclopedia,* by 2000, half of India's Christians were Pentecostal/Charismatic.[1] By now in 2017, the figures should have been increased exponentially as the last decade has seen remarkable growth all over India, especially in north India among the Tribals, Dalits, and lower castes in rural areas as well as among middle class in urban centres. Nevertheless, until recently, the growth and expansion of the movement in India has not been noticed or documented. Even now it is hard to ascertain the extent and pace of its growth and consolidation, however, the recent testimonies and researches have shown that the movement is growing fast.

More and more people from different ethnicities, castes and classes are embracing the movement. The visible signs can be seen in urban centers as well as even in interior villages. Anyone who travels in cities and villages of India can see ample evidences of the growth of Pentecostalism among common masses. Today some of the largest Christian congregations of India are Pentecostal churches, in cities such as Chennai, Bangalore, Hyderabad, Kolkata and New

[1] See, David B. Barrett, George T. Kurian, and Todd M. Johnson, *World Christian Encyclopedia,* 2nd ed. (New York: Oxford University Press, 2001), 360.

Delhi.[2] In South India, the Pentecostal movement has considerable influence among the middle class and urban population and this has resulted in the formation of a number of big churches. For example, in Chennai city itself, two Pentecostal churches claim a membership of 30,000 each, who meet in multiple services, and include people from all walks of life.[3] Similarly, another church in Bangalore boasts of more than 18,000 members.[4] Heavenly Feast, a neo-Pentecostal church that opened in Kottayam, Kerala, ten years ago, has grown to a congregation of more than 10,000 members and claims that about 20,000 people attend their Sunday services.[5]

Although, relatively new, begun in the beginning of the last century with the simultaneous revival movements, the movement has also began to make impact in north India with its influence among the common masses and the down-trodden and carved a niche in the difficult terrains of north Indian mission fields. The North Indian cities have seen the springing up of some big indigenous Pentecostal and Charismatic churches.[6] For instance, an indigenous Pentecostal/Charismatic movement known as *Yeshu Darbar* in Allahabad, Uttar Pradesh claims a gathering of 50,000 people of every caste and religion who were healed and delivered from evil possession.[7]

The influence of the Pentecostal movement can be visible even in small cities and rural areas of north India. My own past 20 years of

---

[2] Chief Editor, "Editorial – Pentecostalism," *Dharma Deepika* 6/2 (July-December 2002): 2.

[3] New Life Assembly of God (AoG) Anna Salai Little Mount, Chennai; for more details see website: http://nlag.in/about_us.htm (accessed 1 March 2012). Another church Apostolic Christian Assembly (ACA), Purasavakkam, Chennai, claims 30,000 members.

[4] Full Gospel Assembly of God Church (FGAG), see website: http://homepage.mac.com/fgag/fgag/ (accessed 1 March 2012).

[5] http://www.theheavenlyfeast.org/about-us.php?pg_id=5 (accessed 1 March 2012).

[6] Roger E. Hedlund, "Indigenous Pentecostalism in India," *Asian and Pentecostal: The Charismatic Face of Christianity in Asia* (Carlisle: Regnum Books International, 2005), 218. Also see Roger E. Hedlund, *Quest for Identity: India's Churches of Indigenous Origin, The "Little Tradition" in Indian Christianity* (Delhi: ISPCK, 2000), 193.

[7] See website: http://yeshudarbar.org/ (accessed 1 March 2012).

experience and knowledge and information from rural areas of north Indian states of Rajasthan, Madhya Pradesh, Gujarat, Maharashtra, Orissa and Bihar has convinced me that many are joining the movement. People from Dalit, tribal and economically poor background embrace the movement as it gives them a new vigour and hope for their lives. In a context of poverty, lack of medical facilities, caste discrimination, social and spiritual oppression, many people find Pentecostal movement as a refuge and a source of strength in their existential struggles.

Having said this, it is important to ask the question why the movement is making such a positive impact in the spiritual and social landscape of India. A cursory glance into the world wide Pentecostal movement gives us the clues that it has certain distinctive features. These distinctive characteristics themselves had played primary role in the origin and growth of the movement. Hence, the history of Pentecostalism can be termed as the continuous replay of these features and we may summarise as follows. Pentecostals attribute great importance to the experience of the Spirit, especially the baptism of the Holy Spirit, a supernatural personal and communal experience along with charismatic gifts which are distinct to the movement. This spiritual experience is considered more important than issues of doctrine and church government. The experience of the Spirit is considered as indispensable for Christian life and mission. It is firmly believed that the Pentecostal church's origin and growth happens only by the powerful work of the Spirit.

Furthermore, another distinctive mark of the Pentecostal Movement is speaking in tongues. Prophecy, interpretation, and other supernatural manifestations of the Holy Spirit are also central to its theology and practice. Pentecostals believe that the coming of the Spirit brings an ability to do "signs and wonders," particularly that of healing and exorcisms.[8] The Indian Pentecostals' strong emphasis on the miraculous and divine healing is a major factor why people are

[8] Johan D. Tangelder, *Azusa Street and Beyond: 100 Years of Commentary on the Global Pentecostal/ Charismatic Movement*, edited by Grant McClung (Gainesville, Florida: Bridges-Logos, 2006).

attracted to its faith and practice in north Indian context.[9] This faith in the charismatic gifts and resultant practices paved way for rapid growth of the Pentecostal movement in the Indian context.

Pentecostals also stress the need of holy life and strongly reject vices such as drinking, smoking, card playing, or other impurities. For them, this strong emphasis on holiness is a vital ingredient of their faith and practice. In fact, separation from the world often becomes an important test of genuine faith. Further, Pentecostals all over the world emphasize the central doctrines of the complete authority of the Bible and the necessity of a conversion experience. They confess that Jesus Christ is Saviour, Sanctifier, Spirit Baptizer, Healer and Coming King. They firmly believe in the sinfulness of human beings, which can only be taken care of through the atoning work of Christ, and the transfer of Christ's righteousness to the believer. Pentecostal theology also stresses the judgment of God, the imminence of Christ's return.[10] These features give uniformity to the movement world over and impetus to its growth.

Along with these spiritual as well as doctrinal positions which certainly give the movement a strong momentum forward, the Pentecostal movement alleviate pains and suffering of the common masses in a unique way of spiritual and social engineering.[11] Even today, as we look into the Indian context, the poor, the vulnerable, lower castes, tribals and women are left to their destiny both by the society and successive governments. The centuries old caste system, racial prejudices, cultural and religious oppression of the Dalits, tribal and women are still continuing. Historically, this century old social systems were further reinforced by colonial powers which facilitated the tiny minority elite groups in acquiring nation's wealth. On the other hand, the majority of the society was deprived of economic, educational and political opportunities. Thus, the poor and vulnerable continued to be powerless and unable to compete with the well off. In such a context, the Pentecostal movement brought a

---

[9] Shaibu Abraham, Ordinary Indian Pentecostal Christology (Unpublished PhD Thesis, University of Birmingham, Birmingham, 2011), 195-206.

[10] Tangelder, Azusa Street & Beyond.

[11] Shaibu Abraham, *Pentecostal Theology of Liberation: Holy Spirit and Holiness in the Society* (New Delhi: Christian World Imprints, 2014).

spiritual dynamic, a revolutionary paradigm shift in the outlook of the deprived. This Pentecostal renewal begins in the innermost core of a human being and according to the Pentecostal understanding, this change happens because of the power of the Spirit. This change impacts totality of a person's life and transformation takes place in physical, economic and social realms.[12] While writing about Pentecostal mission, Young-Gi Hong undergirds the social relevance of the Spirit renewal and Pentecostal movement,

> When Christians are empowered with the Spirit of God they are equipped to do "kingdom works" in the midst of human suffering and need. In many cases, the motivation of many oppressed people to join Pentecostal churches came from the belief that it was a way to social improvement. Pentecostalism started to gather strength precisely among the most disadvantaged or dissatisfied sectors, such as the urban poor, women, and independent middle class groups, because it provided them with a sense of life and hope.[13]

It is clearly demonstrated that the poor and oppressed are being liberated and uplifted once they joined the movement.[14]

As we explore the origin and the history of the movement we will stumble upon the story of ordinary people, the Dalit, tribals, women and the vulnerable became heroes of this movement as a result of this spiritual renewal. The inner renewal they received through the Spirit awakening catapulted them to be vanguard of the movement as well as agents of liberation. The community of believers becomes a catalyst to positive changes in the society by the virtue of

---

[12] Wonsuk Ma, "Asian (Classical) Pentecostal Theology in Context," *Asian and Pentecostal: The Charismatic Face of Christianity in Asia,* edited by Allan Anderson and Edmond Tang (Carlisle: Regnum Books International, 2005), 66-67. To have comprehensive treatment of the positive impact of the Pentecostal movement upon the poor and the vulnerable, see Donald E. Miller and Tetsunao Yamamori, *Global Pentecostalism: The New Face of Christian Social Engagement* (Berkeley, California: University of California Press, 2007).

[13] Young-Gi Hong, "Church and Mission: A Pentecostal Perspective," *International Review of Mission* XC/358 (July 2001): 300.

[14] Abraham, Ordinary Indian Pentecostal Christology, 215-227.

their holiness outlook and Spirit inspired life-style. They desist from every sort of vices rampant in the society and encourage others to follow a new life. Thus, the movement makes both personal as well as social transformations and we see these aspects in the history of the movement.

At the same time, it is also important to notice that Pentecostal movement world over is a movement of great diversity and complexity. In different continents one may see Pentecostals with variety of doctrines and practices.[15] In India also we find different expressions of Pentecostal faith in different regions as well as even in same place.[16] The movement is highly contextual and adaptive to the local cultural practices without compromising its doctrines. As the Spirit drives ordinary church members outwards to share the gospel, so the gospel message becomes contextualized. This contextualization, in part, happens due to the emphasis on experience–linking personal experience and experience of God, the Spirit. This contextualization sometimes contrasts with the official church teaching.[17]

Most of the Pentecostal churches in north India are indigenous and do not have any connection with any western Pentecostal denominations. They are locally oriented and raise their own financial resources for their growth and activities. Pentecostal churches in India are self-propagating, self-supporting and self-governing.[18] Even though, some of the Pentecostal churches are part of worldwide denominations, local congregations are free of any external domination, raise their own resources and free to decide their own mission activities.[19] As we explore into the history of the

---

[15] For example, the Oneness Pentecostal group baptizes in the name of Jesus only and not in the name of the Trinity.

[16] For example, The Pentecostal Mission (TPM) which was formerly known as the Ceylon Pentecostal Mission (CPM) has certain differences in doctrines.

[17] Andrew M. Lord, The Holy Spirit and Contextualization, *AJPS* 4/2 (2001): 204.

[18] Roger E. Hedlund, *Quest for Identity: India's Churches of Indigenous Origin, The "Little Tradition" in Indian Christianity.* Delhi: ISPCK, 2000 and Roger E. Hedlund, 'Indigenous Pentecostalism in India', in *Asian and Pentecostal: The Charismatic Face of Christianity in Asia,* edited by Allan Anderson & Edmond Tang. (Carlisle: Regnum Books International, 2005).

[19] Michael Bergunder, "Constructing Indian Pentecostalism: On Issues of Methodology and Presentation" in *Asian and Pentecostal: The Charismatic Face of*

movement, we find it overwhelmingly diverse in its origin, history and practices.

For this reason, recently, historians, theologians, and religious observers began to consider and critically appreciate historical origin as well as theological and social relevance of the Indian Pentecostal movement.[20] However, the researchers face many inherent obstacles. It is difficult to draw a precise picture of the Pentecostal growth and expansion in Indian context, especially in the north. It spreads across states, different languages and people groups. For a researcher to reach every nook and corner of the country is practically impossible. The difference of languages, cultures and lack of access into interior parts of north India makes the research a difficult exercise. Moreover, there are numerous church movements, para-church and charity organisations working in far flung areas of Indian cities and villages. Many of them are run by individuals or groups unknown in the public. They work silently, spreading the Pentecostal message and doing charitable works among the most disadvantaged people. Besides, there are house churches and people's movement not having a leader or church affiliation but carrying out spiritual activities. Furthermore, on daily basis more and more new churches, mission organisations and individual endeavours are being initiated. Obviously, it is a difficult task to get entire details of such a diverse entity to ascertain its origin and history.

In addition, lack of historical and theological documentation of Pentecostalism in India has made the study of the movement an uphill task.[21] The prominent books on history of Christianity in India written by denominational historians seldom have a mention of the Pentecostal movement as part of Indian Christianity. While

---

Christianity in Asia, edited by Allan Anderson & Edmond Tang (Carlisle: Regnum Books International, 2005).

[20] Allan Anderson, "Revising Pentecostal History in Global Perspective," *Asian and Pentecostal: The Charismatic Face of Christianity in Asia,* edited by Allan Anderson and Edmond Tang (Carlisle: Regnum Books International, 2005), 147-173, especially, 166.

[21] Wonsuk Ma, "Asian (Classical) Pentecostalism: Theology in Context," *Dharma Deepika* 6/2 (2002): 14.

writing the history of Pentecostal movement in Kerala, Pulikottil touches the problem,

> It remains an undisputed fact that in the grand narratives that the historians belonging to the historical churches created, Pentecostalism has not been given due recognition. The elitist historiography presented by the groups that are dominant either by their place in history or political or economic advantage, Pentecostalism and especially Pentecostalism in the non-western cultures did not get the due place.[22]

The movement was earlier considered as either a heresy or an aberration in the Christianity. Added to this, the early Pentecostals did not have the resources or training to write down their origin and history in the academic sense of history writing and this was true until 1990's. Most of them have been more concerned with evangelism, in apocalyptic issues, and even in survival, than in recording and interpreting their history in a professional manner.[23] Now efforts are being made to gather oral traditions, testimonies and written documents and local researches are being carried out to salvage the mission stories and local theologies from the margins. Further, there is awareness among Pentecostals themselves to understand their past and articulate their local theological expressions grown out of its unique peculiarities and context.[24]

---

[22] Paulson Pulikottil, "As East and West Met in God's Own Country: Encounter of Western Pentecostalism with Native Pentecostalism in Kerala," *AJPS* 5/1 (2002): 7.

[23] Stanley M. Burgess, "Pentecostalism in India: An Overview," *AJPS* 4/1 (2001): 98.

[24] Anderson, *Spreading Fires;* Bergunder, *The South Indian Pentecostal Movement.* In Kerala Pentecostal History Saju Mathew has brought up many forgotten pioneers of Pentecostalism; See Saju Mathew, *Kerala Penthecosthu Charithram,* 2nd ed. (Bilaspur, India: Margam Books, 2006); A. C. George, "Pentecostal Beginnings in Travancore, South India," *AJPS* 4/2 (2001).

Nevertheless, to reconstruct the history of Pentecostal movement in its entirety is almost impossible[25] and such efforts have not been quite successful as the pioneers of the movement have failed to keep the records of the actual happenings and the mission ensued subsequently. There are many reasons for such a sorry state of affair. First of all, many of them in the forefront of the movement were illiterate or semi-literate and they had lacked training to document the happenings. Moreover, their burning aspiration and passion to reach maximum number of souls before the imminent return of Christ had proved history-writing as a futile exercise.[26] Besides, the western Pentecostal missionaries who had such training had knowingly or unknowingly left out the valuable contributions of the native pioneers.[27] The common believers, who were real pioneers, who spearheaded the movement, were left out in the peripheries of the history and in the unknown tracts of time.[28] In addition, those who knew at least some of those forgotten heroes and heroines and heroic stories of mission and growth of the movement were all dead.[29] What Frykenberg says is true about Indian Pentecostal history. 'What we call "forgetting," in a collective sense, happens when any community fails to transmit to posterity what its members understand about themselves and events in their past. "Remembering," by enhancing and preserving its own history, is one of the crucial means by which a community empowers itself.'[30] Similarly Anderson also comments, 'The multitudes of nameless people responsible for the grassroots

[25] Ivan M. Satyavrata, "Contextual Perspectives on Pentecostalism as a Global Culture: A South Asian View," in *The Globalization of Pentecostalism*, edited by M.W. Dempster, B.D. Klaus and D. Petersen (Carlisle: Regnum Books International, 1999), 205.

[26] A. Cerillo Jr. & G. Walker, "Bibliography and Historiography of Pentecostalism in the United States," *The New International Dictionary of Pentecostal and Charismatic Movements* (Michigan: Zondervan Publishing House, 2002), 390.

[27] See Allan Anderson, *Spreading Fires: The Missionary Nature of Early Pentecostalism* (London: SCM Press, 2007), 7-9.

[28] Anderson, *Spreading Fires,* 7.

[29] Burgess, "Pentecostalism in India," 98.

[30] Robert. E. Frykenberg, "Christianity in South India Since 1500: Historical Studies of Transcultural Interactions within Hindu-Muslim Environments," *Dharma Deepika* (December 1997), 5.

expansion of the movement have passed into history forgotten and their memory is very difficult to recover.'[31] Even when we find some details, they are to be sifted and arranged so that to make the sense. Likewise, it is essential to read between the lines to get at least a dim picture of the real thing. The foreign missionaries knowingly or unknowingly omitted the names of native missionaries who were in the frontlines of the battlefields. In some cases, racial prejudice also created tensions in the mission.[32] Therefore, it is virtually impossible to dig out all the details of the history of the movement with chronological accuracy. However, it is noteworthy that recent time a reasonably fair account of the history of the south Indian Pentecostalism has come up.[33]

In the north Indian scenario, the history of the Pentecostal beginning and the subsequent expansion of the movement are not adequately documented. As we have explained, the movement had its beginning in multiple centres and different times, many of the stories would have lost forever since no one was there to collect and preserve them. What we have now is the early history of mission (1905-1920 approximately) sketched by Allan Anderson[34] and others[35] deciphering the letters and correspondence of the foreign

---

[31] Anderson, *Spreading Fires,* 8.

[32] Anderson, "Revising Pentecostal History in Global Perspective," 158-160. See Anderson, "Revising Pentecostal History in Global Perspective," 163-165.

[33] See Saju Mathew, *Kerala Penthecosthu Charithram,*; Anderson, *Spreading Fires,* 75-108; Michael Bergunder, *The South Indian Pentecostal Movement in the Twentieth Century* (Cambridge: William B. Eerdmans Publishing Company, 2008); T.S. Samuel Kutty, *The Place and Contribution of Dalits in Select Pentecostal Churches in Central Kerala from 1922-1972* (Delhi: ISPCK, 2000); V. V. Thomas, "Pentecostalism among the Dalits in Kerala from 1909 to the Present: A Subaltern Reading," *UBS Journal* 3/2 (September 2005): 89-94.

[34] Anderson, *Spreading Fires,* 75-95.

[35] See Gary B. McGee & S. M. Burgess, "India," *The New International Dictionary of Pentecostal and Charismatic Movements* (Michigan: Zondervan Publishing House, 2002): 118-126; Stanley M. Burgess, "Pentecostalism in India: An Overview," *AJPS* 4/1 (2001): 85-98; G. B. McGee, "Pentecostal Phenomena and Revivals in India: Implication for Indigenous Church Leadership" *International Bulletin of Missionary Research* 20/3 (July 1996); Gary B. McGee, '"Latter Rain" Falling in the East: Early-Twentieth-Century Pentecostalism in India and the Debate over Speaking in Tongues,' *Church History* 68/3 (1999).

missionaries laboured in the beginning of the movement.[36] To write the history of the north Indian Pentecostalism, we need to trace the history of those forty or more years between 1920 and 1960 and make historical connections, which is hard to retrieve. The generation who knew those parts of the Pentecostal history has already died. Again, the history afterwards of 1960 is also difficult to track, as the missionaries did not document what they have done. But it is noteworthy that A.C. George has given an account of the history of the Assemblies of God churches in India which also includes North India.[37] However, there are many other Pentecostal churches and organisations and pioneers whose stories are to be collected and displayed. What we have today is the biographies and autobiographies of some Pentecostal leaders which can be hagiographical in nature and very often over emphasise the personal achievements. Thus, the reconstruction of the Pentecostal history in north India is infested with myriad of difficulties and odd challenges such as dearth of authoritative sources and overemphasis on certain individual leaders. We need to depend on the testimonies of those people who have definite memories about the events that had happened in the past. Here the challenge a researcher faces is to check the veracity of oral traditions and stories narrated by Pentecostal believers. The option available before us is to collect those stories people tell us which they have heard from those who have died some years before and sift them to retrieve the historical events. Therefore, care has to be taken to sketch an unbiased and objective picture.

The history of Pentecostalism in north India is the history of Pentecostal mission and the Church growth movement. It is the encounter of the Gospel with the religio-cultural and socio-political contexts of India. It is the story of the Spirit movement; *the bright wind of the Spirit* blowing all over the Indian subcontinent; the story of Spirit-filled people who faced the powers of darkness; of their triumphs and failures, joys and sorrows, unity and division, love and hate, their partnerships and even clashes; of divine and human elements working together.

---

[36] Anderson, *Spreading Fires,* 9-13.

[37] George, *Trailblazers for God.*

As the Pentecostal churches in India continues to grow, especially in north India, and as the Indian theological endeavours also evolve rapidly, it is vital to reconstruct the lost history of the movement to hand it over to the future generations. The Pentecostals must recognize their own historicity, the fact that we are ourselves a part of history, not only a product of past history but also a potential agent for history in the future. We are linked to the past and to the future in the present. Now is the time to correct omissions and distortions in Pentecostal historiography.[38]

The readers need to note that the non-availability of primary sources of many of the missions and churches that originated in the north have resulted in not mentioning them in this work. Some of them do not disseminate their details owing to the current north Indian situation of opposition and persecution. Moreover, many of the missions mentioned are begun by south Indian missionaries as they have disseminated information through biographies and websites. It is to be noted that the mission organisations and church movements mentioned here are not entirely classical Pentecostal type only; many of them are of charismatic or neo-Pentecostal/ Charismatic in nature, albeit one way or other we can find some Pentecostal connections in most of the entities explored here. Many of the leaders of these north Indian movements have their background formation in Pentecostalism and its doctrines and practices and these Pentecostal traits amply reflected in their statement of faith and mission practices.

Thus, in the following pages, we shall try to unravel the stories of the Pentecostal movement in north India and the people who spearheaded the movement. I cannot claim to bring out an accurate picture of the events and developments that had begun a century ago and continued in the subsequent decades. Again, I am not claiming to be totally objective and precise. More than two decades of my life and exposure in north India and close association with the movement make me somewhat confident to approach the subject. On the other hand, my theological journey and rigorous academic training enable me to approach this task with caution and objectivity. It is a modest

[38] Deborah Kaye Cole, "Historiographic Approaches to Asian Pentecostalism," *AJPS* 9/1 (2006): 62.

effort to glance into those eras to have a glimpse of at least some of the events to get a taste of what had happened. It is anticipated that this endeavour will do some justice to those forgotten men and women of faith and also infuse a sense of courage and self confidence to the north Indian Pentecostal movement in a context of opposition and hostility.

Chapter 2

North Indian Pentecostal History Methodological Considerations

Before we attempt to explore the history of the north Indian Pentecostal movement, it is vital to understand that the history writing in the recent years have been drastically changed and we need to be aware of the way in which we need to approach the past. This is important as we may not leave out any events or people as well as to have an objective description of history. Earlier leaders of the movement wrote their stories of exploits as the history of the movement. These stories are known as "hagiographies," which do not consider the hard work of grass-root heroes. Recently, the Pentecostal historiography has undergone major shifts; it looks at what is now popularly known, "history from below" or "subaltern history" or "history from the edges," which we need to discuss before we see the history itself.

Methodological Shift in Pentecostal Historiography

The centre of gravity of Christianity has shifted from global north to global south. In this shift, the Pentecostal movement has played a dominant role.[1] It is assumed that within coming few decades Pentecostal churches which are independent and indigenous will

[1] Allan Anderson, "Revising Pentecostal History in Global Perspective," *Asian and Pentecostal: The Charismatic Face of Christianity in Asia,* edited by Allan Anderson and Edmond Tang (Carlisle: Regnum Books International, 2005), 151.

represent a far larger segment of global Christianity.[2] Earlier it was conceived that the Pentecostalism was the product of North America and was exported to the end of the earth and Burgess calls it as 'Amerocentric historiographic assumptions.'[3] Pentecostal histories that are Euro-centric in nature describes Pentecostal history beginning with the Topeka revival and gaining momentum at the Azusa Street Mission and spreading all over the world.[4] Whatever growth had happened in the mission fields were attributed to the foreign missionaries because administration as well as finance was in their hands. Native workers and believers who had toiled day and night were not counted worthy enough to be mentioned. According to these histories the heroes and heroines are westerners regarded as the main role players responsible for the global expansion of Pentecostalism.[5] This sort of history was produced by some Pentecostal scholars who used uncritical and hagiographical tradition to prove that Pentecostal beginning was common within their churches. Such tradition is called as the 'providential approach,' on the belief that Pentecostalism was a spontaneous, providentially generated end-time religious revival.[6]

However, the magnificent and dynamic growth of the Pentecostal movement worldwide, especially in the third world, has forced Christian historians, especially Pentecostal historians, to rethink the methodology of Pentecostal history writing.[7] Now Pentecostal historians speak about multi-centred or poly-centric

---

[2] Philip Jenkins, *The Next Christendom: The Coming of Global Christianity* (Oxford: Oxford University Press, 2002), 7-8.

[3] Stanley M. Burgess, 'Pentecostalism in India: An Overview,' *AJPS* 4/1 (2001): 85-86.

[4] Paulson Pulikottil, "As East and West Met in God's Own Country: Encounter of Western Pentecostalism with Native Pentecostalism in Kerala," *AJPS* 5/1 (2002): 7.

[5] Anderson, "Revising Pentecostal History in Global Perspective," 158-159.

[6] Agustus Cerillo Jr., "Interpretive Approaches to the History of American Pentecostal Origins," *Pneuma* 19/1 (Spring, 1997): 30-32; Cerillo Jr. & Walker, 'Bibliography and Historiography of Pentecostalism in the United States, 397-399; In the case of American Pentecostal historiography they have outlined four approaches, namely, the providential approach, the genetic approach, the multicultural approach and the functional approach.

[7] Anderson, *Spreading Fires*, 4-13; Anderson, "Revising Pentecostal History in Global Perspective," 147-173, especially 166.

origin of Pentecostalism rather than Topeka or Azuza Street origin. For instance, Everett A. Wilson rightly identifies the issue:

> Since 'Pentecost,' as early enthusiasts referred to their collective experience, had several beginnings, the problem is to decide which of the claimants should take title to the distinction. But multiple subsequent 'outpourings' demonstrate that in any event, no claim can be made to exclusivity.[8]

Similarly Allan Anderson also questions the notion of North-America as the 'Jerusalem' or origin of Pentecostalism and speaks about many 'Jerusalems.' "There were many 'Jerusalems:' Pyongyang, Korea; Beijing, China; Pune, India...Pentecostalism has many varieties, and not just the North American classical Pentecostal kind."[9]

Today historians began to read 'history from below' rather than 'history from above;' history taken from the perspectives of the poor and powerless rather than the rich and the powerful.[10] This is known as 'subaltern historiography' which seeks to restore a balance highlighting the role of ordinary and poor in the making of history. This history is recorded from the memory and lips of ordinary Pentecostal believers. Therefore it is an oral history. Moreover, oral history is a history built around people. It allows heroes not just from leaders but also from unknown majority of the people. It offers a challenge to the established myths of the history and provides a

---

[8] Everett A. Wilson, "They Crossed the Red Sea, Didn't They?: Critical History and Pentecostal Beginning" in *The Globalization of Pentecostalism*, edited by M.W. Dempster, B.D. Klaus, D. Petersen (Carlisle: Regnum Books International, 1999), 91.

[9] Anderson, "Revising Pentecostal History," 153.

[10] Anderson, *Spreading Fires*, 4-13; Anderson, "Revising Pentecostal History in Global Perspective," 147-173, especially 166; Bergunder, *The South Indian Pentecostal Movement in the Twentieth Century*, 11-14; Michael Bergunder, "Constructing Indian Pentecostalism: On Issues of Methodology and Presentation," *Asian and Pentecostal: The Charismatic Face of Christianity in Asia,* edited by Allan Anderson and Edmond Tang (Carlisle: Regnum Books International, 2005), 188-191.

radical transformation of the social meaning of history.[11] Therefore, primary task is to retrieve the local traditions from those who are still alive and remember and to be recorded for future generations.[12]

Moreover, the documentary sources of Pentecostal history outside the western world available are the letters, reports, periodicals of western Pentecostal missionaries. They were mainly meant to harness financial and prayer support from North America and Europe. These sources mostly talk about the activities of western missionaries and the official positions of power and privileges of their authors, leaving behind the native workers who were foot-soldiers of mission. Therefore, Anderson asserts, "The Pentecostal experience of the power of the Spirit was the reason for the unprecedented flexibility on the part of its emissaries to the various cultures into which the Pentecostal message was taken. But historiographical imperialism and ethnocentrism of the past must be rectified."[13] Such a high handedness in history writing has distorted the real face of the movement and often made many voiceless and nameless.

This has resulted in lack of documentary evidences of even later happenings and makes the reconstruction of the history challenging and arduous. Here we face a daunting task of digging out the scanty and fragmentary information and stories to place them to see what had actually happened. Therefore, we need to 'read between the lines' to get those left-behind heroes and their stories. This is certainly a hazardous task, since the possibilities of misinterpretation become greater with incomplete information, especially in the case of those who have already died and whose voices have been lost. Moreover, the 'reading between the lines' may cast some Pentecostal missionaries in less favourable light.[14] Likewise, we must 'listen to the margins' to hear the subdued voices of real heroes of the movement. Anderson rightly points out,

---

[11] Paul Thompson, *The Voice of the Past: Oral History*, 2nd ed. (New York: Oxford University Press, 1988), 1-18.

[12] Anderson, "Revising Pentecostal History in Global Perspective," 159.

[13] Anderson, "Revising Pentecostal History in Global Perspective," 166.

[14] Anderson, "Revising Pentecostal History in Global Perspective," 158-159.

> The revising of the history of Pentecostalism in the twenty-first century must be undertaken, not by emphasizing the missionary 'heroes' of the powerful and wealthy nations of the world, but by giving a voice to the people living in the world's most marginalised parts. We must listen to the margins by allowing the hitherto voiceless and often nameless ones to speak, and by recognising the contribution of those unsung Pentecostal labourers of the past who have been overlooked in our histories and hagiographies.[15]

Now in Pentecostal historiography oral traditions are being gathered to salvage the 'mission stories from the margins,' although with limited success.[16] With this in our mind it is significant to form a Pentecostal historical methodology for north India before we explore the actual historical events ensued as a result of intense mission activities so that we may approach the past with objectivity.

Methodology for North Indian Pentecostal History

Taking the cues from the above discussion that a new approach to the history writing is the norm today, it is important to have a number of deciding factors while we explore the history of north India. Besides, the north Indian context is entirely different from south India. Again the formation and growth of the north Indian Pentecostal movement greatly differ from that of south Indian Pentecostalism. Therefore, we need a unique approach which would encompass as many as possible areas such as political, social, religious and economic contexts to be included in the history writing. These vital aspects will enable us to construct a fair and balanced historical account, which could be used as a methodological framework for the writing of North Indian Pentecostal history. This will also help us to dig out the forgotten stories of heroes and heroines who were real trailblazers in the mission fields in order to do some justice to their hard work. Moreover, this methodological frame may also

---

[15] Anderson, "Revising Pentecostal History in Global Perspective," 166.

[16] Anderson, *Spreading Fires;* Bergunder, *The South Indian Pentecostal Movement in the Twentieth Century;* For Kerala Pentecost history, see Saju Mathew, *Kerala Penthecosthu Charithram,* 2nd ed. (Bilaspur, India: Margam Books, 2006).

give insight and further impetus to those who involve in the task of writing of the north Indian Pentecostal history in the future.

Poly-centric Historical Approach: Local and Regional Histories

First of all, while attempting to shape a history of the north Indian Pentecostal movement, it is essential to look into the *local* and *regional* histories. This is because Pentecostalism in India, especially in the north is not a single monolithic structure originated in a particular centre but sprang up from different contexts, in different times and by the works of different people.[17] What W.R. Shenk says is apt here; we must develop a 'polycentric' idea of church history, considering the 'missionary and indigenous dynamics' of church growth.[18] Besides, north India consists of more than 20 states with diverse languages, culture and geography and there exist many indigenous independent Pentecostal and charismatic churches and organisations. It is important to look into each state and geographical location to fully understand the origin and growth of the movement. We may find a set of separate category of happenings, stories, denominations and pioneers in each place. Hence, writing a Meta-history connecting all these states and denominations is certainly impossible. Of course, there are churches of south Indian origin like the Indian Pentecostal Church (IPC) or the Sharon Fellowship Church or branches of the Assemblies of God (AoG) or the Church of God (CoG) which are world-wide Pentecostal denominations in almost all states of north India. Nevertheless, even their beginnings in north Indian states were attributed to unique events and leadings and their growth were contributed by further deciding factors later stages.

It is also important to notice the fact that there are hundreds of smaller church groups and mission organisations under individuals and groups working in remote villages and smaller towns. Moreover, there are charitable institutions such as orphanages, old age homes and medical missions under Pentecostal banner but not related to

[17] Satyavrata, "Contextual Perspectives on Pentecostalism as a Global Culture: A South Asian View," 207.

[18] Wilbert R. Shenk, "Introduction," *Enlarging the Story: Perspectives on Writing World Christian History*, Wilbert R. Shenk (ed.), (Maryknoll, NY: Orbis Books, 2002), xi.

any mainline Pentecostal denominations. Further, there are house churches and small groups which make considerable influence among people and contributed to the Pentecostal growth. Therefore, a researcher needs to look into all these entities and keep in mind that attempting to write a history of Pentecostalism in north India is actually writing of multiple histories.

Religio-Cultural and Socio-Political Context

Secondly, it is crucial to consider the religio-cultural and socio-political context of north India which is unlike the south. In the south, especially in Kerala state, a sizeable Christian community had existed when Pentecostalism entered in the horizon in beginning of the 20th century. These Christians claimed their origin to Saint Thomas, the disciple of Jesus Christ.[19] Even though they had a theology and liturgy, the members of these churches did not have a mission theology or missionary activities. Nevertheless, people of other religions like Hindus knew what Christianity was, and indeed its practices were. At the time of the advent of Western evangelical missionaries, main denominations were Roman Catholics and Syrian Orthodox churches. According to Paulson Pulikottil, the Syrian Orthodox Churches would have experienced revivals, as they did not hold to a cessation theory with regard to the charismata.[20]

In the 18th to 20th centuries, most of India was ruled by European powers especially the British. This opened avenue for many protestant mission organisations to send their missionaries.[21] These missionaries carried out self-help programmes and other charity works. There was emphasis on education and social reformation by missionaries as

[19] A. Mathias Mundadan, *History of Christianity in India Vol. 1, From the Beginning up to the Middle of the 16th Century (up to 1542)* (Bangalore: Theological Publications in India, 1984).

[20] Paulson Pulikottil, "Emergence of Indian Pentecostalism," *Dharma Deepika* 6/2 (July-December 2002): 47-48.

[21] According to Lamin Sanneh, missionaries compounded the nature of foreign domination by showing racial prejudices and aligning with colonizers which was often transferred into the ecclesiastical realm. Lamin Sanneh, "World Christianity and the New Historiography," *Enlarging the Story: Perspectives on Writing World Christian History,* Wilbert R. Shenk (ed.), (Maryknoll, NY: Orbis Books, 2002), 100-101.

well as awakened natives. These activities enabled many Christians as well as lower caste people who were under crushing poverty to join western missionaries. Protestant missionaries who came from the Welsh Revival, the Keswick Convention or the Pietistic Movements had led the native Christians to appreciate biblical ideas and created a spiritual hunger for personal development. Besides, some revivals had already taken place and at least some of the people were familiar with 'Pentecostal-like' experiences.[22] News of revivals in different parts of the world also generated anxious anticipation among native Christians. Thus, when Pentecostal missionaries reached India, Kerala became fertile ground for the Pentecostal mission and many churches were established.

However, the north Indian situation was entirely different. Even though the Mukti revival was so prominent and powerful (which we will discuss later), the effects of this revival did not materialise in widespread Pentecostal church planting as in the south. After few years, the movement became stagnant and native missionaries were not able to withstand the hostile situation of north India. Consequently, the Mukti Revival did not contribute in terms of Pentecostal church growth.[23] Even today, the small town where the revival took place does not have any Pentecostal activities or established Pentecostal denominations.[24] According to Hollenweger, in 1963 even the Mukti Mission leadership claimed they were totally ignorant of the Pentecostal revival.[25] The north Indian condition was detrimental

---

[22] See G. B. McGee, "Pentecostal and Pentecostal-like Movements (1860-1910)" in *The New International Dictionary of Pentecostal and Charismatic Movements,* edited by Stanley M. Burgess (Michigan: Zondervan Publishing House, 2002), 118-119. Also see G. B. McGee, "Pentecostal Phenomena and Revivals in India: Implication for Indigenous Church Leadership" *International Bulletin of Missionary Research* 20/3 (July 1996), 112-114.

[23] Anderson, *Spreading Fires*, 88.

[24] Even today, the people around the small town where the revival took place (Kedgaon, about 60 km from city of Pune) do not know about Pentecostalism. I have visited the Mukti mission centre twice few years back (2000 and 2004) and asked people around the town about Pentecostalism; however, most of the local people do not know what it is.

[25] Walter J. Hollenweger, *Pentecostalism: Origins and Developments Worldwide* (Peabody, MA: Hendrickson, 1997), 120; see the footnote 11; This is conveyed by

to the spread and growth of Pentecostal movement because of the cultural and religious barriers. Therefore, it is significant to look at the religio-cultural context of 19th and 20th centuries.

Hinduism in north India was strong enough to resist the overtures of Pentecostal missionaries. The religion and cultural pattern of the north Indian society, family bonding and strong communal boundaries acted as dampening aspects. Besides, the caste consciousness among the Hindus and the widespread misapprehension that Christianity is the religion of beef-eaters and lower caste acted as impediments to the Pentecostal growth. The local religious forces were against the propagation of the gospel and vehemently opposed the mission activities. Even today situation is not so different.

Further, Christian missions had sparked a reformation among Hindus. This reformation took essentially in two ways. Some began to bring a renaissance among the educated and elite Hindu population by condemning and trying to abolish evil practices like *Sati* (burning wife in the funeral pyre of husband), child marriage, idol worship and such superstitious practices. For instance, Raja Rammohan Roy who is known as 'the father of Indian renaissance' was instrumental in bringing many such reforms in Indian society. The second strand was in defensive mode, emphasised to going back to old traditional practices such as idol worship, polytheism and superstitions. Some others like Swami Dayananda Swaraswati rejected idolatry but began a movement called back-to-Vedas.[26] This branch of thought became more militant and formed organisations like *Arya Samaj* which later became a catalyst in the formation of militant organisation like RSS.

The socio-political scene in the last part of 19th century and beginning of 20th century also need to be considered. The dominant feature of this period was the western colonialism, predominantly of the British. It is significant that the western imperialism and the Christian missions came together and it seemed that they support

G. Fletcher, Superintendent of Ramabhai Mukti Mission in a letter dated 21-3-1963 to Hollenweger.

[26] Sunand Sumithra, *Christian Theologies from an Indian Perspective* (Bangalore: Theological Book Trust, 1995), 17-19.

each other, though they were often in sharp disagreement. This created a view among the average educated Hindus that Christianity as the faith of the oppressors. For instance, Mahatama Gandhi, in his famous Motihari speech, in Bihar declared that the foreign missionaries were good people, who came to serve the people of India and had nothing to do with the colonial rulers after his secret stay with the missionaries in Motihari mission house. In spite of all these, the foreign missionaries were considered to be part of the colonial forces and all their philanthropic activities were resisted by the public. The gospel could not make much inroad in north Indian context and the response was very poor. Only a few people, mostly the orphans and uprooted people, became Christians as a result of the long years of hard labour by the missionaries.

Furthermore, Western imperialism was the catalyst which facilitated the emergence of a nationalistic spirit which resulted in the formation of various movements like the 'Non-cooperation', 'Self-rule', and 'Quit-India', 'swadeshi' (use of only India-made goods and products) movements.[27] These political movements rejected whatever were related to western imperialism, misconstruing Christian faith as something of western product. Besides, the Hindus looked down upon Christianity as the religion of *mlechhas* (the pagans) and even today some think the same and more militantly organised manner.[28] Thus, the North Indian situation was much harder than its southern counterparts. Therefore, the Pentecostal history of North India must be written taking these contexts into account.

Subaltern History

In north India the major Pentecostal growth had been among tribal, dalits and lower caste people. They were living in the peripheries of the societies and considered as untouchables. They were suffering from social ostracism and caste cruelty, utter poverty and various illnesses and demonic oppression. Therefore, churches of indigenous origin such as Pentecostal movements utilised practices of healing

---

[27] The *Sepoy Mutiny* in 1857 was the first spark. Later in 1885 this desire of self rule resulted in the formation of Indian National Congress and the subsequent freedom movement.

[28] Sumithra, *Christian Theologies from an Indian Perspective*, 8.

and exorcism.[29] The Pentecostal message of bodily healing and empowerment in the Spirit attracted them. As Allan Anderson argued, the healing ministry was one of the most potent instruments of Pentecostalism worldwide[30] and it was true in the growth of the movement among the poor masses of north India. Additionally, those early adherents found a new freedom and equality in the Pentecostal community which did not exist in their religion and culture. Given the above social and cultural inequalities and oppression, it is worth focusing on the movement as an instance of social protest just as Robert Anderson shows; however, it would be a mistake to equate 'ecstatic religious experience' of Pentecostals as a 'surrogate for success in the social struggle.'[31] They were the expressions of local people who were marginalised and oppressed. The growth of the Pentecostal movement was the result of social protest of oppressed local people.[32] The spiritual and social impact of the movement created a liberative momentum among the subaltern and they embraced the Pentecostal message overwhelmingly. Moreover, women, the most vulnerable of the society, were being given equal space in the movement. They could stand along with men and spread the message of hope to their counterparts in the society.

Therefore, we need to reconstruct a 'history from below' to appreciate the actual impetus for the movement. According to Frykenberg, the Subaltern reconstructions of history tend to deconstruct all previous perceptions of history and assume that they are deficient. The constructions claimed are those of 'popular memory' or 'oral traditions.' These are drawn from below, with only occasional resort to hitherto despised or yet untouched colonial documents and other previously neglected documents.[33] Therefore, there is a great need to understand the historical consciousness of the

---

[29] Hedlund, *Quest for Identity*, 11.

[30] Anderson, *Spreading Fires*, 35-42.

[31] Robert M. Anderson, *Vision of the Disinherited: The Making of American Pentecostalism* (New York: Oxford University Press, 1979), 149.

[32] See Hedlund, *Quest for Identity*, 9.

[33] Robert E. Frykenberg, *History and Belief: The Foundations of Historical Understanding* (Michigan: William B. Eerdmans Publishing Company, 1996), 294.

natives and 'listening to the margins' intently.[34] We need to ask what sort of historical memories do they carry and how this consciousness came about. For a historian who tends to overlook those existential struggles and memories of the people may miss the 'real history.' As Pulikottil says, 'Pentecostalism is (still) the religion of the subalterns in most parts of the world; they are not the subjects of their history.'[35] Hence, it is essential to explore the mission works among the poor masses giving special reference to healing ministry and works of the Spirit like exorcism while writing the north Indian Pentecostal history.

Local Revival Movements

Another important aspect of the Pentecostal history in north India is the revival movements that have occurred in different places in various times. Many of them were sporadic and often isolated in nature. These revivals were not imported from any Western nations or by any missionaries but spontaneously happened as local people prepared themselves for the events. These revivals took place in different locations and different times with different languages, seldom having connections with one another. People in the forefront of these revival events were common people, some even uneducated, however, they became powerful leaders to lead the people in spiritual fervour. Ordinary women were stepped into the leadership by the virtue of the Spirit empowerment and became trailblazers. In some cases, hundreds of people altogether had been baptised and churches were established.[36]

---

[34] Ronald N. Bueno, "Listening to the Margins: Re-historicising Pentecostal Experiences and Identities," in *The Globalization of Pentecostalism*, edited by M.W. Dempster, B.D. Klaus, D. Petersen (Carlisle: Regnum Books International, 1999), 268-288.

[35] Pulikottil, "As East and West Met in God's Own Country..."

[36] For instance, in Vyara, Gujarat (1970), one of the meetings by Shanmukh Patel became a place of great outpouring of the Spirit. He claims that, within seven days, he had baptised almost 3,500 people there and that, in his lifetime, he baptised more than 38,000 people. Shanmukh Patel, interview, Pipal Kuah, 10 August 2009.

However, these were not like the mass conversion took place earlier with the foreign missionaries as groups of people decided to join Christianity.[37] There were powerful manifestations of the works of the Spirit like healings, exorcisms, prophecy and many confessing their sins with loud cry. Then these people began to take the revival fire into nearby villages and towns and churches began to grow. Moreover, such revivals are not a one-time event, but rather repeat again and again in different locations. Wilson rightly comments, 'Revivals last not because the movement had an impressive beginning, but rather because periodic renewal keeps the enthusiasm vibrant despite energy-sapping generational, organisational and circumstantial changes.'[38] Therefore, the challenge before historians and those who involve in Pentecostal research in north India is to unearth these local revivals arose in various regions and localities. It is not only going to help us reconstructing the real Pentecostal history, but will also lay a strong foundation for Pentecostal theology and missiology.

Role of Native Missionaries

In shaping the north Indian Pentecostal history, it is imperative to highlight the role and hard works of north Indian native missionaries.[39] As already mentioned, the history of Pentecostalism in India, especially in the north is the history of the encounter of gospel message with different people-groups like dalits, tribals, lower castes and the poor in their religio-cultural, economic and socio-political contexts. That is, it is a mission history. While writing about the changing task of Christian history, Mundadan asserts that the history of Christianity is the 'history of the impregnation of these contexts by the gospel, the assimilation of the cultures of the peoples by the gospel and that of the gospel by their cultures, and the history of the consequent changes in the Christian movement and

---

[37] F. Hrangkhuma, "Factors that Contributed to the Arrest of Mass Movements Towards Christianity in India," *Christianity in India: Search for Liberation and Identity,* edited by F. Hrangkhuma (Delhi: ISPCK, 2000), 312.

[38] Wilson, "They Crossed the Red Sea, Didn't They?," 92.

[39] Allan Anderson argues that it is imperative to highlight the leading role and hard work of local Pentecostal leaders and missionaries while writing Pentecostal history anywhere in the world; Anderson, *Spreading Fires,* 5-9.

of the cultures of the people.'[40] However, this has not happened as western historians earlier thought: from western countries to the rest of the world. It was by the Spirit movements in different locations in various times and by ordinary people. Anderson rightly observes that Pentecostal movement's emphasis on the empowering ability of the Spirit to equip ordinary believers for missionary service without requiring prior academic qualifications, Pentecostalism was probably more dependent on 'national workers' than any other missions.[41] Women also had played crucial role in the Pentecostal mission and the church growth. They exercised the charismatic gifts and had the freedom to spread the gospel message.[42] Therefore, the postcolonial historiography does help us to look at particular historical events from the perspectives of the natives.[43]

However, the earlier histories of Pentecostal movement written by western missionaries usually begin with American pioneers like Parham or Seymour and in the case of India, Albert Garr and George Berg.[44] In a similar fashion, today we can find some biographies, reports and testimonies of north Indian church growth written in terms of south Indian ascendancy and flavour. This is because, just as in the beginning of the Pentecostal movement in India the foreign missionaries were controlling the administrative and financial set up, many of the mission organisations and churches in north India

---

[40] A. Mathias Mundadan, "The Changing Task of Christian History," *Enlarging the Story: Perspectives on Writing World Christian History,* Wilbert R. Shenk (ed.), (Maryknoll, NY: Orbis Books, 2002), 23.

[41] Anderson, *Spreading Fires,* 7.

[42] Michael Bergunder, "Women and Leadership in the South Indian Pentecostal Movement," *Dharma Deepika* 6/2 (July-December 2000): 35-40; Although, Bergunder writes about south-Indian Pentecostalism, it true to north-Indian Pentecostalism also; Anderson, *Spreading Fires,* 4.

[43] Paulson Pulikottil, "As East and West Met in God's Own Country: Encounter of Western Pentecostalism with Native Pentecostalism in Kerala," http://www.pctii.org/cyberj/cyberj10/paulson.html (accessed January 10, 2010).

[44] Anderson, *Spreading Fires,* 6; Anderson also comments: Pentecostalism is not a movement that had a distinct beginning in the USA or anywhere else...it is a movement or rather a series of movements that took several years and several different formative ideas and events to emerge. Pentecostalism then as now is a polynucleated and variegated phenomenon.

are also being controlled by the south Indian Pentecostals, especially from Kerala who have financial resources, infrastructure, and secular as well as theological education. Moreover, some of the native workers in the beginning were not recent converts from Hinduism or tribal religion or Dalit background, but were already Christians in denominational churches,[45] as in the case of Kerala Pentecostalism in the beginning of 20th century.

On the other hand, in north India, Christianity and colonialism are considered synonymous by those who advocate the Hindutva Ideology. The Hindutva understanding reasons that Christianity was brought to India by the colonial powers and alleges that the message and method of missionary work of the native Indian Pentecostal churches are in continuity with that of the colonial missionaries. For them, the native missionaries are agents of the colonialism getting huge financial resources to convert gullible poor masses. Therefore, it is imperative to establish the native character of Pentecostal mission in the construction of north Indian Pentecostal history.

Western Missionary Movements

As already discussed, the western missionary movement has played a definite and crucial role in the growth of Pentecostal movement. Even though north India was a hard place for foreign missionaries in terms of climate, culture, language and strong anti-western feeling because of colonial rule in India, many missionary organisations played major role in presenting gospel to the north Indian people.[46] The people who were attracted to these missions were mainly dalits, tribals and poor people. Many had embraced Christianity by the efforts of missionaries in medical and educational realms and also by the monetary relief provided to the poor. Moreover, dalits and other lower castes found Christianity as a religion which could liberate them from the caste oppression. It is also need to remember that at least some of the western missionaries had racial prejudice and

[45] For example, Shanmukh Bhai Patel who was a pioneer in the revival in Gujarat and Maharashtra was working among Church of North India (CNI) and Brethren Churches; Shanmukh Bhai Patel, interview by author, Pipal Kuah, Gujarat, 10 August 2009; Anderson, *Spreading Fires,* 4

[46] McGee, "Pentecostal Phenomena and Revivals in India," 124.

did not allow the native leadership to come up. Even worse, in the beginning some were not interested in lower caste people embracing Christianity.[47] For instance, one missionary wrote to the Board of Foreign mission that the coming of low cast as 'raking in rubbish into the church.'[48] Nevertheless, later many of them did convert and missionaries made extra efforts to teach them the Bible and to encourage them to pursue education.

When the Pentecostal missionaries entered the scene, only a few Christians existed in the north. Many who embraced the Pentecostal faith in the beginning were these converted Christians. Further, many Pentecostal missionaries targeted the existing missionaries, who knew local languages and customs, so that they may later spread the Pentecostal fire. This resulted in the formation of Pentecostal networks and spreading of Pentecostalism in rapid pace.[49] Many who received Pentecostal experience or were thrown out from their parental mission bodies due to a different outlook began to develop their own Pentecostal mission. These independent missionaries purchased properties and opened mission stations in larger cities along the railroad lines to facilitate evangelism. However, north India proved to be hardest mission field and missionaries could not make considerable foray into cast-ridden and superstitious minds of the people.[50] Then, early Pentecostal missionaries concentrated on establishing philanthropic institutions.[51] Thus, it is important to ponder the contributions of both western non-Pentecostal

---

[47] James Massey, "Christians in North India: Historical Perspective with Special Reference to Christians in Panjab," *Religion and Society* XXXIV/3 (September 1987), 99-102, see especially 101. Massey says that in the beginning the missionaries were interested only in preaching the Christian gospel to high caste people.

[48] James Massey, "Christians in North India," 101.

[49] Anderson, *Spreading Fires*, 90.

[50] McGee, "Pentecostal Phenomena and Revivals in India," 124.

[51] McGee, "Pentecostal Phenomena and Revivals in India," 124. The AG has the most extensive system of institutional networks such as an orphanage and girl's school at Bettiah; a girl's orphanage at Purilia; the James Harwey Boys" school at Nawabganj; a leper work at Uska Bazar, begun in 1911 by Minnie Abrams; the "Baby Fold" at Rupaidiha; a girl's industrial school at Siswa Bazar, etc., the best known AG work is in Calcutta, "Mission of Mercy" which now feeds over 20,000 hungry people every day, a hospital, a school of nursing, a junior college, a vocational

and Pentecostal missionaries in the history of north Indian Pentecostalism.

South Indian Contributions

Another important aspect we need to consider is the contributions of South Indian Pentecostals to North Indian Pentecostalism. After the 1940s western missionaries both non-Pentecostal and Pentecostal found it difficult to stay back in India and began leaving India because of the Indian Freedom movement. Many of them left to their native places. Thus, whatever negligible Pentecostal works carried out in north India came to a standstill. However, by the time, many spirit-filled Pentecostal missionaries from Kerala began to move towards north India. Most of them were poor, having no financial support, and even not knowing Hindi or any other north Indian languages.[52] Nevertheless, their zeal was such that they ventured into the unknown to disseminate the Pentecostal message and to liberate many from the clutches of oppression, both spiritual as well as social. They came to the places where there was some Christian presence and instilled biblical teachings of believers' baptism, Spirit-baptism and the importance of a holy life among the existing Christians who were converted by western evangelical missionaries. With their help the south Indian Pentecostal missionaries moved into the un-evangelised villages and towns and began to establish churches. Later missionaries from Tamil Nadu also began their mission in north India. Consequently, several Pentecostal denominations came into existence. Therefore, it is

---

school, six village clinics, a hostel for destitute youth, a drug prevention program, and 12 schools that provide instruction for 6,000 children.

[52] The stories of M.K. Chacko, Kurian Thomas, K.V. Philip, Thomas Mathews, proves this fact; see M.K. Chacko, *An Autobiography* (Delhi: Pastor M.K. Chacko, 1976); Thomas Thonnakkal, *Marubhoomiyile Appostalan* [The Apostle of the Desert: A Biography of Thomas Mathews] (Udaipur, India: Cross and Crown, 2004); Thomson Thomas Kaithamangalam, *Marubhoomiyil Thalarathu* [Not Tired in the Desert: A Biography of Thomas Mathew] (Udaipur, India: Cross and Crown Publications, 1996); Roger Simmons, *Vision Mission and a Movement: The Story of Dr. Thomas Mathews and the Native Missionary Movement* (Richardson, TX: Native Missionary Movement, 2008; Kurien Thomas, *God's Trailblazer in India and around the World* (Itarsi, India: Kurien Thomas, 1986).

essential to look into the contributions of south Indian missionaries in the history of north Indian Pentecostalism.

Simultaneously, we also require considering what Bergunder says 'the existence of historical connections and synchronous interrelations' between Pentecostal denominations existing in the north and south. According to him, both these criteria have to be applied as Pentecostalism is a global movement.[53] This is also true in the case of north Indian Pentecostalism, as the south Indian Pentecostalism has influenced the worship, doctrine and life-style of north Indian Pentecostals. Furthermore, it is also important to focus on churches that have split and on pastors who formed their own denominations by splitting the churches they were part. 'It is precisely these friction,' comments Bergunder, 'that are most important for the historian who tries to sketch a diachronous network.[54] The main problem with this approach is that 'it is not in line with the common stereotyped pattern of testimonies and hagiographies that church leaders like to tell.'[55] Therefore, to write a Pentecostal history, we must trace these historical connections, which are hard to get in oral testimonies or written documents. According Bergunder, it will never be possible to reconstruct the full diachronous connections; hence, historian needs to break up the sources and apply hermeneutical suspicion.[56]

Mission Organisations

Another noteworthy aspect need to consider is the works of hundreds of Para-church mission organisations[57] like 'Operation Mobilization' (OM), India Every Home Compassion and Jesus Calls of D.G.S. Dinakaran in Chennai so on. They have done marvellous missionary

[53] Bergunder, "Constructing Indian Pentecostalism," 189. Also see Bergunder, *The South Indian Pentecostal Movement in the Twentieth Century,* 12-13.

[54] Bergunder, *The South Indian Pentecostal Movement in the Twentieth Century,* 12-13.

[55] Bergunder, *The South Indian Pentecostal Movement in the Twentieth Century,* 12-13.

[56] Bergunder, *The South Indian Pentecostal Movement in the Twentieth Century,* 13.

[57] Satyavrata, "Contextual Perspectives on Pentecostalism as a Global Culture: A South Asian View," 207.

works almost all parts of north India, through distributing tracts, Bibles, radio evangelism and other gospel literatures. Many of the members of these organisations were spirit-filled Christians who had burning passion for north India. Through them many people had come to know about Christianity and the Pentecostal experience. They directed these new contacts mostly to Pentecostal churches, thus highly contributing to the already existing Pentecostal works.

Global Influence

Lastly, it is vital to consider the global influence upon the north Indian Pentecostal movement and its history. As already seen, in the beginning of the movement, the western Pentecostal missionaries were active in the forefront of the movement. Even though later missionaries have gone back, the bonds remained. Many of the north Indian Pentecostal churches have partnership with Pentecostal churches in western countries in terms of ministry and in some cases for financial resources.[58] Moreover, recently the neo-Pentecostal movement and charismatic movement have tremendous impact upon the north Indian Pentecostal movement in its worship style, theology and practices especially in urban centres. Some of the evangelistic and missionary methods of western neo-Pentecostals are being used by Pentecostal churches in India, even though their effectiveness is still to be ascertained.

Hence, it is crucial to take these factors while attempting to write a history of north Indian Pentecostalism. These aspects would enable us to unearth what is unknown and unsaid and keep a sensible balance in portraying what is somewhat known. This methodological frame work will remind us of some of our biases, prejudices and oversights and help us to chart our course of history writing in right track. These elements would enable us to high light the achievement of the marginalised, uneducated and women folk who did not get their due place in the annals of history. Therefore, while looking into the history and growth of north Indian Pentecostalism we will consciously attempt to highlight these factors so that a reasonable and fair picture may be drawn out.

---

[58] Satyavrata, "Contextual Perspectives on Pentecostalism as a Global Culture: A South Asian View," 206.

Chapter 3

North Indian Pentecostal History Background

In this chapter we will briefly glance into the background in which the Indian Pentecostalism had it origin and growth, especially the north Indian Pentecostal movement. This is very important because the Pentecostal movement whether it is in the south or north did not originate in a vacuum or as some historian earlier considered as "providentially" began. Both the south Indian and north Indian Pentecostal movement had a strong affinity with the Christian strands existed before their origin. The Indian Pentecostal movement was actually an off-shoot of larger Christianity existed in the south and north even though we find a definite break in several aspects of the movement. It was similar to the first century Christianity which came out of Judaism and became a revival movement world over still retaining some of the former characteristics and leaders. More importantly, the north Indian Pentecostal movement had unbroken connection with the south Indian Christianity as well as south Indian Pentecostalism as we have seen in the methodological consideration for north India.

This background study will also help us to make "synchronous" and "diachronous" connections advocated by Bergunder and make sense of the stories emerge in our exploration. As we have noted, many of the earlier north Indian leaders were from south Indian Christian background and their Syrian Christian background positively and negatively impacted the movement in the north. Some of the north

Indian Pentecostal churches like IPC or others have directly come from Kerala Pentecostal movement. Additionally, some of the north Indian leaders, churches and missionary organisations were either split from these south Indian churches worked in the north or still having some south Indian traits in them. Therefore, before we go into the actual Pentecostal history, we will look at the history of Christianity as a whole in India and also in north India which would enable us to situate the north Indian Pentecostal history in the context and give us some historical specifics in which the movement has been grown. But here we are not able to go into the subject matter in details as it is not warranted in this effort and there are number of well researched books available on both the south Indian and north India Christianity. What we do here is to just give a glimpse of the historical development of Christianity in few pages to make better historical connections while we discuss the north Indian Pentecostal history.

Christianity in South India

Indian Christianity is as old as the Christianity itself. The tradition of St. Thomas is the base of the history of the Christian churches in Kerala. It is believed that one of the disciples of Jesus, Saint Thomas came to Kerala in 52 A.D. by sea, converted a few high caste Hindu families. Then he visited China preaching gospel, returned to India, and organised the Christians of Malabar and established churches in Kodungallur, Niranam, Palayur, Nilackal, Kollam, Kokamangalam, kottakavu etc., in Kerala.[1] Then he moved to Coromandal, and suffered martyrdom on or near the Little Mount, today's Chennai and his body was brought to Mylapore and was buried there.[2] This is

[1] Varghese Perayil, *The Oath of Coonan Cross* (Adoor, Kerala: Kerala Study Centre, 2007), 1.

[2] There are certain stories prevalent among the Christians in Kerala regarding some of the miraculous feats of Thomas in relation to the establishment of Christianity. In Palayur, the place where one of the churches he established, he watched the Brahmins performing their morning Sun worship (*Surya Namaskaram*) in a temple pond, throwing water up towards the Sun. St. Thomas asked them to bid water stay in the air, as a sign of the power and truth of their religious ceremony. The Brahmins tried to perform as Thomas asked but could not do that. But Thomas

known as Malabar tradition. This tradition also says that Christians from Malabar, West Asia and even from China used to go on pilgrimage to Mylapore.[3]

However, according to Firth, there are no written records regarding these traditions.[4] There are various opinions and arguments among the historians the veracity of the traditions and stories prevalent among Syrian Christians in Kerala.[5] The Malabar tradition is mainly of oral tradition like folk songs and stories[6] and most of the Indian church historians vehemently support the Indian tradition.[7] The archaeological evidence of trade between the Roman Empire and India in the first century A.D. adds credibility to this tradition. The fact that John, Bishop of Persia and Great India, was one of the

---

took some water and threw it in the air and commanded it to stay in the air in the name of Jesus and it happened. The tradition says that seeing this miracle, these Brahmin families were become Christians and Syrian Christians of Kerala claim the family lineage of these initial Christians.

[3] A. Mathias Mundadan, *History of Christianity in India, Vol 1, From the Beginning up to the Middle of the 16th Century (up to 1542).* (Bangalore: Theological Publications in India, 1984), 29; V. Titus Varghese & P.P. Philip, *Glimpses of the History of the Christian Churches in India* (Madras: The Christian Literature Society, 1983), 5. According to the western tradition, Thomas followed the well established trade routes by land and reached India by the middle of the first century. He preached the Gospel in Parthia and India, converted many people to Christianity, including some members of royal family and suffered martyrdom in India and was buried in India.

[4] Mundadan, *History of Christianity in India,* 29.

[5] C.B. Firth, *An Introduction to Indian Church History* (Delhi: ISPCK, 1976), 3-14. Like Firth some of the western historians like Basnage, Tillemont, La Croze, James Hough, Sir John Kaye question the validity of these traditions; see D. Arthur Jeyakumar, *History of Christianity in India: Selected Themes* (Delhi: ISPCK, 2004), 11.

[6] Here, we are not able go into all the details as this work does not allow to discuss the vast subject matter. See Samuel Hugh Moffett, *A History of Christianity in Asia: Beginnings to 1500, Vol.1.* 2nd Rev. ed. (New York: Orbis Books, 1998), 25-36; also see Mundadan, *History of Christianity in India,* 29-66; A. Philipose, *The Apostolic Origin and Early History of the Syrian Church of Malabar* (London: The Christian Literature Society, 1904); Gérard Garitte & J. N. Farquhar, *The Apostle Thomas in India according to the Acts of Thomas* (Kottayam, Kerala : [s.n.], 1972).

[7] The songs like *Thomas Rabban Pattu, Margam Kali Pattu, Veeradian Pattu,* etc. (Pattu means Songs).

signatories in the Acts of the council of Nicea (325 A.D.) shows that by 3rd century there existed a strong Christian community in Kerala.[8] A bishop is known to have been sent from Jerusalem to India in 345 A.D. and a traveller in 530 A.D. reported the presence of Christian communities in the southwest and in Ceylon.[9] The Syrian Christians of Kerala still hold on to this tradition.

In 1498 A.D. when the Portuguese arrived in Kerala, they found a vibrant Christian community.[10] However, the Portuguese considered Syrian Christians as superstitious and tried to convert them into Catholic fold. Roman Catholic Church began determined effort to win the *Syrian* Christians aided by Pope Leo X in 1514 with *Padroado* which gave to the Portuguese rights over the Christians of the East.[11] This policy had resulted in Synod of Diamper in 1599 in which with the honourable exception of 30,000 *Syrian* Christians, all submitted to Rome.[12] Later, the native Christians realised that they had lost their status and identity and revolted against the Roman Catholic domination. This resulted in an open rebellion known as *Coonan Kuris* (the Bent or Crooked Cross) where thousands of St. Thomas Christians gathered in a church in Cochin and holding a long rope attached to a cross swore a solemn oath to abjure their loyalty to foreign Catholic archbishop in 3rd January 1653.[13] These

---

[8] Indian church historians like E.M. Philip, K.N. Daniel, etc., support the south Indian tradition; see Jeyakumar, *History of Christianity in India*, 10-11.

[9] F. Hrangkhuma, "Church in India" *Church in Asia Today: Challenges and Opportunities,* edited by Saphir Athyal (Singapore: Asian Lausanne Committee for World Evangelism, 1996), 400.

[10] P. Thomas, *Christians and Christianity in India and Pakistan* (London: George Allen & Unwin, 1954), 31.

[11] Samuel Hugh Moffett, *A History of Christianity in Asia: 1500-1900, Vol. II* (New York: Orbis Books, 2005), 4-8.

[12] Robin Boyd, *An Introduction to Indian Christian Theology* (Madras: Christian Literature Service, 1969), 7.

[13] See Boyd, *An Introduction to Indian Christian Theology*, 7-8; Perayil, *The Oath of Coonan Cross;* Joseph Thekkedath, *History of Christianity in India, Vol. II, From the Middle of the Sixteenth Century to the Seventeenth Century* (Bangalore: Theological Publications in India, 1982), 64-90; Moffett, *A History of Christianity in Asia: 1500-1900,* 13-16; Varghese & Philip, *Glimpses of the History of the Christian Churches in India*, 33-37.

stories tell us the existence of the Syrian Orthodox Church as well as the Catholic Church in Kerala. This feeling of *syrianness* has encouraged Kerala Pentecostal leadership to assert their freedom and form independent movement.[14]

Contemporaneous to above episodes, another form of Christianity reached in Indian shore, the Protestant mission with the Dutch and the British colonisers. However, the foreign merchants had purely commercial interest in India and did not allow any missionary works. The first protestant missionaries from Europe reached in India were two young Germans, from Pietistic Movement, Bartholomaeus Zieegenbalg and Heinrich Plutschau in Tranquebar (Tamil Nadu) in 1702, which can be considered as the beginning of Protestant mission in India (Danish-Halle Mission).[15] Later in 1760 the Moravian missionaries reached in Tranquebar and their missionary endeavours produced much greater impact in south Indian mission, followed by other English missionary organisations such as LMS, CMS and so on.[16] As we will see later, these missionary agencies became instrumental in preparing appropriate background for the great life-changing revivals in the later decades which resulted in the formation of Pentecostal movement in Kerala.

Meanwhile by the Anglican influence a schism broke out in the Syrian Orthodox church after 1850's in the leadership of reformist Abraham Malpan and a group of Syrian Christians formed a new church in 1888-1889, named as *Mar Thoma Church.* Its growth was accelerated by a series of revivals in next few decades and it is famous for its convention in Maramon, the river-bed of Pampa River in Kerala.[17] Later in 1919, western missionary churches of varying traditions such as Anglican, Methodist, Congregationalist, Presbyterian, and Reformed had begun discussions to form union at Tranquebar. This resulted in the formation of the Church of South

---

[14] Perayil, *The Oath of Coonan Cross;* Moffett, *A History of Christianity in Asia: 1500-1900,* 17-19; Thekkedath, *History of Christianity in India, Vol. II,* 91-96.

[15] Pulikottil, 'Emergence of Indian Pentecostalism, 54. Also see Pulikottil, 'As East and West Met in God's Own Country; http://www.pctii.org/cyberj/cyberj10/paulson.html (accessed January 10, 2010).

[16] Moffett, *A History of Christianity in Asia: 1500-1900,* 236-242.

[17] Moffett, *A History of Christianity in Asia: 1500-1900,* 242-246.

India in 1947 which is known as CSI. But the Lutherans, the Baptist and other smaller evangelical churches remained independent.

Having said this, the initial leaders and key members of the Kerala Pentecostal movement were from these historic churches. With the cooperation and financial assistance of foreign Pentecostal missionaries they began to disseminate the Pentecostal messages all over Kerala and other south Indian states. As we have seen the foreign missionaries had problem with local languages and culture. Therefore, the Kerala Christians were in the frontiers of mission and evangelism. Besides, many of these new adherents of Pentecostalism had secular education and social standing in a caste ridden society at those times. They also had a good knowledge of the Bible and revival experience which they have attained from their former churches. Some of them were actually spiritual leaders in their respective churches and looking for a vibrant Christian spirituality and true biblical Christianity. When foreign Pentecostal missionaries introduced the Pentecostal message, these people could readily identify and assimilate it, as they already had those experience and understanding. It is to be noted that some of these key leaders or leaders trained by the initial leaders of Kerala Pentecostalism became initial Pentecostal missionaries in north India and through them the movement began to grow.

Christianity in North India

Some historians have attributed the genesis of north Indian Christianity to St. Thomas, another tradition prevalent which is known as western tradition derived from *Acts of Thomas.* It says that Apostle Thomas reached in India following the trade routes, in the middle of the first century in the kingdom of King Gundaphar (now in Punjab state). Thomas introduced himself as an architect and the king asked him to build a palace for him and gave him lot of money. However, Thomas distributed the money to the poor and later when the king came to see the palace, Thomas took him to the places where he gathered the poor people of the kingdom to be cared for. The king was angry and imprisoned him. But later Thomas was released as king's brother had a dream where he saw a palace built in heaven by Thomas. Then Thomas converted members of royal families and others, suffered martyrdom in India and was buried. Later his mortal remains were transferred to Edessa.[18]

However, the present conditions in north India do not show any sign of Christian presence as in Kerala. We find mention of some Roman Catholic Jesuits who had been invited by the Moghul Emperor Akbar (1556-1605 A.D.) and founded churches for who had migrated to the major urban centres of the empire. But there were not more than forty converts from Islam in Agra in 1604. The most of the Christians of north India consisted of converts from Hindu origin, especially of the poor and lower castes.[19]

It is the arrival of William Carey, the Baptist missionary, who is known as 'the father of the modern missionary movement', in 11th November, 1793 which unleashed protestant mission in North India, especially in Bengal and surrounding regions. Carey and his friends, Joshua Marshman and William Ward, known as 'Serampore Trio' were not allowed to work in Calcutta by the English, hence they moved to the Danish colony of Serampore (near Calcutta) in 1799. Subsequent years have seen great missionary expansion in terms of people attracted to Christianity, translation of the scripture, social reforms and education. Before his death on 4th June 1834 Bible had been translated into more than 30 languages.[20]

Later, missionaries of Anglican, Scottish, Presbyterian, Lutheran, American Presbyterian and American Methodist worked in different parts of north India. According to James Massey, these missionaries failed to identify with the local people or culture. In the beginning most of them were not interested in the poor or lower castes as they considered themselves far superior to the natives.[21] Besides, the majority of Christians were the product of Christian mass movements

---

[18] See K.T. Joy, *The Mar Thoma Church: A Study of its Growth and Contribution* (Kottayam, Kerala: Good Shepherd Press, 1986), 92-100.

[19] Mundadan, *History of Christianity in India,* 25-26; Moffett, *A History of Christianity in Asia: Beginnings to 1500,* 25-36; Varghese & Philip, *Glimpses of the History of the Christian Churches in India*, 6.

[20] Thekkedath, *History of Christianity in India, Vol. II,* 441-447; Moffett, *A History of Christianity in Asia: 1500-1900,* 23-25.

[21] Moffett, *A History of Christianity in Asia: 1500-1900,* 255-274; Massey, "Christians in North India," 94-96.

of dalits and lower castes in different parts of north India, not by the foreign missionary efforts but by the works of local people. These movements were taken place primarily in Punjab, Uttar Pradesh, Bihar and West Bengal.[22] James Massey terms them as 'Spirit Movements.'[23] Massey comments, 'It was the direct intervention of God himself through his Spirit where missionaries turning their faces from these poor and lowly, and at every moment God was working among these forsaken and were turning them toward the missionaries.'[24] However sociologically speaking, such mass movements were in reaction to caste-system, especially untouchability and also for social and economic upliftment.[25]

In north India some of the above mentioned churches began unity effort to form a Church Union in 1929 like south India. After many years of negotiations and consultations the Church Union in North India was inaugurated on 29 November, 1970 in Nagpur. Today these missionary churches is known as 'the Church of North India' (CNI), the communion of six Christian Churches of North India.[26] There are also other protestant denominations like Lutheran, Mennonite, and Presbyterians, and so on remained independent.

Same as in Kerala, in the beginning of the movement a good number of people from these churches joined Pentecostal movement. There were a number of revivals occurred among these churches in different places and times as happened in the south. These initial

---

[22] See Massey, "Christians in North India," 102-104.

[23] See F. Hrangkhuma (ed.), *Christianity in India: Search for Liberation and Identity* (Delhi: ISPCK, 2000).

[24] James Massey, "Christianity among the Dalits in North India with Special Reference to Punjab," *Christianity in India: Search for Liberation and Identity,* edited by F. Hrangkhuma (Delhi: ISPCK, 2000), 1-13.

[25] Massey, "Christians in North India," 104; Also see Moffett, *A History of Christianity in Asia: 1500-1900,* 420-425; see D. Arthur Jeyakumar, "Group conversion Movements to Christianity in the Indian Sub-Continent," *Indian Church History Review* XXXIX/2 (December 2005): 63-73; W.W. Jones, "Mass Movement as Missionary Dream and Reality," *Indian Church History Review* XXVIII/2 (1994): 135-151.

[26] S. Albones Raj, "Mass Religious Conversion as Protest Movement: A Framework," *Religion and Society* XXVIII/4 (1981): 58-66; S.L. Parmar, "The Church in North India," *Ecumenical Review* XX/1 (January 1968): 74.

leaders were the people who experienced those revivals and also having ministry experiences. Their former Christian experiences enabled them to lead from the forefront. These people along with the south Indian Pentecostal missionaries began to foray into cities and villages as they were familiar with languages and customs. Thus, the combined work of both the south Indian Pentecostals and north Indian local leaders enabled rapid growth of the movement. Even today, those Pentecostal churches and missions having local people in the forefront have been showing greater growth than the south Indian missionaries working alone. People from downtrodden background delivered through Pentecostal message are more eager to proclaim this liberative message to their kith and kin who are in the same predicament. That is why Dalits, tribals, women and the downtrodden people flock into Pentecostal churches in north India. With this background we shall look briefly into the Indian Pentecostal history in general and north Indian Pentecostal history in particular. Here it is to be noted that the Pentecostal history India is the history of revivals occurred in the twentieth century and the mission and church growth followed. In the following chapters we shall explore these revivals and the subsequent rapid growth of the movement in north India.

Chapter 4

North Indian Pentecostal History (1906-1920)

The Pentecostal history in India can be termed as the history of revivals among the native people and the rapid mission ensued subsequently through the common believers. These revivals had their origin among the native Christians and its influence was far-reaching. 'India played an important role in the worldwide revival that took place in the first decade of the twentieth century, especially through the events in the Khasi Hills and at the Mukti Mission,' comments Bergunder.[1] Obviously, the harbinger of the formation of Indian Pentecostal churches in north India can be attributed to the revival movements in the last century. In the following pages we shall briefly survey the revivals which had influenced some way or another in the formation of Pentecostal churches in India as a whole and north India in particular.

Twentieth Century Revivals in India

The second of half of nineteenth century and the beginning of twentieth century had seen a series of revivals worldwide. They created a heightened spiritual momentum among the Protestant churches and fervent mission activities. It was also true in Indian context and India had witnessed a number of powerful revival movements that changed the spiritual landscape of India forever.

---

[1] Bergunder, *The South Indian Pentecostal Movement in the Twentieth Century*, 23.

Revivals in South India

The precursor of the Pentecostal movement in south India can be traced back to a number of revivals that broke out in Kerala in denominations like Mar Thoma Church and churches run by CMS in 1860, 1873 and 1895. It was John Christian Aroolappen of Tirunalveli, in the state of Tamil Nadu in south India, who was became instrumental in the revival. He was a local catechist trained by Carl T.E. Rhenius, a Prussian missionary sent by the Church Missionary Society in 1814 who worked in Tamil Nadu until his death in 1838. Aroolappen was also tutored by Anthony Norris Groves, an independent missionary from England who had arrived in India in 1833 and been greatly influenced by the millennialism and other teachings of the Plymouth Brethren.[2] Aroolappan happened to read about the revivals in the US, England and Ulster in 1857-59 and greatly inspired by them and earnestly prayed for a movement of the Spirit in India.

It was reported that a mighty revival broke out on March 4, 1860 and the outpouring of the Spirit was accompanied by prophecy, glossolalia, glossographia, interpretation of tongues and intense conviction of sins among nominal Christians. There were dreams, visions, signs in the heavens, and people falling down and/or shaking.[3] This revival resulted in passionate evangelistic activities among the native people, which were neither supported by missionaries nor by western money. There was flood of conversions, which amazed western missionaries who were really struggling to educate the masses and to convert them.[4]

G.H. Lang's report, based on Aroolappen's diary, shows that like other Pentecostal revivals there were months of preparation, which included prolonged prayer, preaching on holiness, weeping

---

[2] See G. B. McGee, "Pentecostal and Pentecostal-like Movements (1860-1910)" in *The New International Dictionary of Pentecostal and Charismatic Movements,* edited by Stanley M. Burgess (Michigan: Zondervan Publishing House, 2002), 118.

[3] See G. B. McGee, "Pentecostal and Pentecostal-like Movements (1860-1910)," 118-119. Also see G. B. McGee, "Pentecostal Phenomena and Revivals in India: Implication for Indigenous Church Leadership" *International Bulletin of Missionary Research* 20/3 (July 1996), 112-114.

[4] G. B. McGee, "Pentecostal Phenomena and Revivals in India," 113-114.

and confession of sins before the actual outpouring of the Spirit. Aroolappen's diary has details of the outbreak of the revival. According to him, from the fourth of May 'the Holy Ghost was poured out openly and wonderfully' upon the congregations.[5] Aroolappen states that although 'some tried to quench the Spirit' the work of the Holy Spirit continued even in other nearby villages, and people began to speak in tongues, interpret and prophesy.[6] This revival lasted for five years and made some impact upon the existing Christian churches. One of the contributions of the revival was that CMS church became a missionary church. The baptism of the Spirit filled the members of Aroolappen's church 'with a holy enthusiasm; and caused them to go everywhere preaching the gospel, in demonstration of the Spirit and of power.'[7]

Along with the above revival, another revival broke out in nearby Travencore, in the state of Kerala in 1873 through a disciple of John Aroolappen, named Mathai (*Pandikaran Mathai Upadeshi*) and others, among CMS and other historic churches in Kerala. He came to Kerala with construction workers and preached in many places of the central Travancore. His evangelistic meetings had created intense conviction of sins and a renewed interest in the Bible reading among the Syrian Christians. Phenomena such as "flinging the arms in the air, shaking in every limb, violent contortions, falling on the ground and rolling about" were noted in these revivals and people also spoke in tongues. This revival also inspired a "Six Years' Movement" in which adherents anticipated the imminent return of Christ. The prominent leaders of these revivals were Kudarapallil Thommen, Rev. Yustus Joseph, a Brahmin convert to CMS, and some others. This revival had continued for more than three years and later waned away.

However, the revival had wider consequences; a section of the clergy and the lay people within the traditional Syrian Christians

---

[5] George Henry Lang, *The History and Diaries of an Indian Christian (J.C. Aroolappen)* (London: Thynne, 1939), 143.

[6] Lang, *History and Diaries*, 145.

[7] G. B. McGee, "Pentecostal and Pentecostal-like Movements (1860-1910)" in *The New International Dictionary of Pentecostal and Charismatic Movements,* edited by Stanley M. Burgess (Michigan: Zondervan Publishing House, 2002), 113.

of Travancore longed for reforms within the Church. The leading clergy who spearheaded the reform movement were Mathews Mar Athanasius and Thomas Mar Athanasius (Mathaikutty and Yakobkutty). They tried to lead the Church on the path of reform emphasizing the reform formulas "Grace alone, Christ alone, Bible alone and Faith alone." When their effort failed to bring about the desired results, in 1889, they left their mother Church to form a new Church, which is now known as the Mar Thoma Church.[8]

Later more radical reforms were advocated by some others, such as believer's baptism, holy life and biblical teachings and these reforms resulted in the formation of the Brethren Church. This movement was called as *separatist* by others. Thus, predominantly Christian population in central Travancore became a fertile ground for Pentecostal seed to grow rapidly.[9] These revival movements paved the way for Pentecostal movement in South India.

Other than these revivals, there were two more revivals in Kerala in the years 1895 and 1908, prior to the coming of western Pentecostal missionaries. These revivals also witnessed similar signs of Spirit movement occurred in earlier; people were being filled with the Holy Spirit, speaking in tongues and other Spirit manifestations such as healings and visions.[10] K.E. Abraham, one of the founding fathers of India Pentecostal church (IPC) states in his autobiography that as a nine year old boy he participated in the 1908 revival and witnessed the power of God manifested in many people, but he did not realize what it was.[11] According to him, this revival took place before George Berg, the American missionary from the Azusa

---

[8] A.C. George, *Trailblazers for God: A History of Assemblies of God in India* (Bangalore: SABC, 2004), 32.

[9] A better description of this revival by Sadhu Kochukunju of Idayaranmula who was also a prominent figure in Marthoma Church is given in a Malayalam Pentecostal Weekly called Maranatha Voice; Muthapackal Kochukunju, "Malankara Kanda Maha Unarv" (Malayalam) (The Great Revival that Saw Malankara) *Maranatha Voice* (October 10, 2006): 8-9, 14.

[10] George, "Pentecostal Beginnings in India," 43.

[11] K.E. Abraham, *Yesukristhuvinte Eliya Dasan*, 3rd ed. (Kumbanad, India: K.E. Abraham Foundations, 2001), 12.

Street Mission came to India in 1908.[12] The people did not have the scriptural knowledge to understand this experience in terms of Holy Spirit baptism, accompanied by speaking in tongues, until Berg arrived from North America.[13] Interestingly these revivals did not have any connection with western Pentecostalism. The leaders as well as ordinary people who were involved in these revivals later associated with western Pentecostal missionaries and established churches in south India. Most of the Pentecostal missionaries travelled to north India were off-shoots of these revival movements.

Revival in Northeast India

Just as in South India, the ground was prepared for the revival in North of India. According to McGee, in 1880-1882, Methodist missionaries toured the land for the promotion of the holiness. "Both Holiness and Higher Life currents flowed through India" says McGee.[14] When the news of revival in Wales reached in India, there were expectations in many quarters. In late 1897 leaders of various mission agencies in India issued a special call to prayer for the conversion of the country.[15] According to Snaitang, this revival needs to be seen in the larger context of pietistic-evangelical Christianity in the 19th century, tribal renascent movement and Christian indigenous movements.[16] The hard work of various western mission agencies in the areas of education, medical service, theological teachings have

---

[12] Abraham, *Yesukristhuvinte Eliya Dasan,* 62-63. Earlier George berg came to India as Brethren missionary but in February 1908 he returned as a Pentecostal missionary with the Spirit experience. See, Anderson, *Spreading Fires*, 95.

[13] Abraham, *Yesukristhuvinte Eliya Dasan*, 86-88.

[14] Gary B. McGee, "Latter Rain" Falling in the East: Early-Ttwentieth-Century Pentecostalism in India and the Debate over Speaking in Tongues,' *Church History* 68:3 (1999), 649.

[15] For instance, the 1898 Keswick Convention in England prayed for the missionary efforts in India by the special appeal of Pandita Ramabai that God would raise up 200,000 Indian evangelists. See G.B. McGee, "Pentecostal and Pentecostal-like Movements (1860-1910)" in *The New International Dictionary of Pentecostal and Charismatic Movements,* edited by Stanley M. Burgess (Michigan: Zondervan Publishing House, 2002), 119.

[16] O.L. Snaitang, "The Indigenous Pentecostal Movement in Northeast India," *Dharma Deepika* 6/2 (July-December 2002): 5.

enabled many tribal people to leave their primal religious rituals to embrace Christianity. The pietistic kind of spirituality led them to have the early Christian spirituality of the first century which contributed to the revival.[17] The Welsh missionaries brought out the translation of the Bible and encouraged people to read and preach. They instructed people that the Bible to be the supreme authority in the matters of faith, ethics and daily life. The preparation of local leadership by missionaries to be appointed as school teachers and evangelists too contributed to the revival. According to Snaitang, the formation of Christian indigenous movements and leadership such as the Home Mission in 1900 led to the rise of indigenous awareness among the Christians. The formation of the Church of God in 1902 attributed to native missionary enterprise and leadership played vital roles in the origin of this revival.[18]

A revival began in March 1905, among tribal people in the Khasi Hills in the northeast India. The preparation for a spiritual awakening began with evening prayer meetings at Mawphlang in the Khasi Hills of central Assam to seek an outpouring of the Holy Spirit throughout Khasi and the entire world. The revival was first experienced during the Presbytery meeting at Pariong in the west Khasi Hills, and spread to Mizoram and Korea in the following year.[19] The believers began to confess their sins and participate in passionate worship and even probably spoke in tongues. The revival in the Presbyterian Church had several elements of Pentecostal expressions such as praying aloud, singing, dancing, trembling and being slain in the Spirit.[20] McGee observes that in contrast to many other revivals, this revival had no prominent person involved.[21] Snaitang believes that the Khasi Revival had a connection with the 1904 Welsh Revival as Christianity in the Khasi Hills had its root in Welsh

[17] Snaitang, "The Indigenous Pentecostal Movement in Northeast India," 6.

[18] Snaitang, "The Indigenous Pentecostal Movement in Northeast India," 6.

[19] T. Nongsiej, "Revival Movement in Khasi-Jaintia Hills," in *Churches of Indigenous Origin in Northeast India,* edited by O. L. Snaitang (Delhi: ISPCK, 2000), 32-34.

[20] Snaitang, "The Indigenous Pentecostal Movement in Northeast India, 7; Also, see, McGee, "Latter Rain" Falling in the East, 652.

[21] McGee, "Pentecostal Phenomena," 114.

Presbyterian mission.[22] It is reported that at least some missionaries initially disapproved the revival, as people began jumping for joy, but later changed their minds as the revival transformed the Christians and many new people came to Christ.[23] 'Therefore,' comments Snaitang, 'the outbreak of the revival movement might well be seen as a significant harbinger for the gradual rise and development of Pentecostalism in Northeast India.'[24]

Revivals in North India

A series of revivals occurred in various parts of north India that impacted the origin of the north Indian Pentecostal movement. Just as in the south these revivals were also occurred among the native people without any intervention from western Pentecostal missionaries. However, it is also to be noted that these revivals did not materialise into wider church growth as experienced in the south.

The Mukti Revival

The expectation of a revival had grown in Mukti Mission at Kedgaon, near Pune, founded by Pandita Ramabhai, a Brahmin widow who was baptized in 1883 and dedicated her life to ministering to Indian girls and women, especially those who were most vulnerable to neglect and abuse in society. There was a famine in India and the Mukti mission had sheltered many women from villages, especially child-widows. In 1898 she attended a Keswick convention where she asked the assembled to pray for 200,000 Indian women and men to carry the gospel to their non-Christian neighbours. She led prayer services among the residents of her Mukti Mission, and organized them into "praying bands" to undertake evangelistic campaigns in the surrounding villages. Inspired by the 1904 Welsh Revival, the prayer band of Mukti Mission, consisted of orphan girls and child-widows, had been praying for an outbreak of revival in India from the beginning of 1905. The number of girls joined for prayer numbered about 500. In June 29, it was said that power of the Spirit manifested

---

[22] Snaitang, "Indigenous Pentecostal Movement," 7.

[23] J. Edwin Orr, *Evangelical Awakening in South Asia*, 113.

[24] Snaitang, "The Indigenous Pentecostal Movement in Northeast India," 7.

like fire so much so that people ran for water to quench the fire. Minnie Abram, who worked with Ramabhai narrates the experience of one of the senior girls at Mukti received the "baptism of fire:"

> The young woman sleeping next to her awoke when this occurred, and seeing the fire enveloping her, ran across the dormitory, brought a pail of water, and was about to dash it upon her, when she discovered that the girl was not on fire. In less than an hour nearly all of the young women in the compound gathered around weeping, praying and confessing their sins to God.[25]

Edith Blumhofer points out that "three features seemed ubiquitous in this Indian revival: fire (felt and seen), intense joy, and public confession of sin."[26] There was also shaking of the body, visions, dreams and coming under the power of the Spirit. Those who received the visitation of the Spirit were all ordinary women, orphan children and child-widows. Moreover, revival created evangelistic fervour among the recipient of the power of the Spirit. Minnie Abraham wrote, 'Some who have sought the baptism of the Holy Ghost and fire have received the fire only for cleansing, but from Acts 2 we see that the tongue of fire gave power for service, as well as cleansing.'[27] Ramabhai explained the revival as the means by which the Holy Spirit was creating a contextual form of Indian Christianity and working in harmony with the Indian psyche to suit their nature and feelings.[28]

The Mukti revival flames spread to other places like Mumbai, Pune, Dhond, Aurangabad, Yeotmal etc. Ramabhai took a band of

---

[25] Minnie F. Abrams, The Baptism of the Holy Ghost and Fire, Kedgaon: Mukti Mission, 1906, 5-6.

[26] Edith L. Blumhofer, "Consuming Fire: Pandita Ramabai and the Global Pentecostal Impulse," in *Interpreting Contemporary Christianity: Global Processes and Local Identities*, edited by Ogbu U. Kalu (Grand Rapids, Michigan, William B. Eerdmans Publishing Company, 2008), 223.

[27] Quoted by McGee, "Latter Rain" Falling in the East, 653; See Helen S. Dyer, (comp.), *Revival in India, 1905-1906* (Akola, Maharashtra: Alliance Publications, 1987), 37-49.

[28] Anderson, *Spreading Fires*, 85.

Spirit-filled helpers to Pune and began a series of meetings in which the Methodist Boy's School was specially blessed. Blessing also came to the Zenana Training home of Miss Soonderbhai Powar, an Indian woman working like Ramabhai. Whole of the school, about 120 girls were in a state of revival. Similarly, the Boy's Christian Home at Dhond, run by Albert Norton also experienced a revival.[29] According Allan Anderson, it is unlikely that Azusa Street has any influence on the Mukti revival. Moreover, there was a tendency among foreign missionaries even from the beginning to discount the revival at the Mukti mission as non-Pentecostal owing the reason that there was no tongue-speaking phenomenon in the beginning of the revival.[30] Unfortunately, Ramabhai and the Mukti mission as an institution later backed out of the Pentecostal movement and interpreted the revival as part of the larger evangelical awakening in the first decade of the twentieth century.[31] It should be mentioned here that even though the Mukti revival impacted many individuals and groups, the movement did not gather momentum in Mukti itself so as to become a part of the classical Pentecostal movement in India.[32] Moreover, as mentioned earlier the Mukti revival neither resulted in church growth nor contributed further in establishment of the north Indian Pentecostal movement.

The Dholka Revival (Gujarat)

Similarly, Dholka town of Ahmadabad district in Gujarat State also experienced a powerful revival. Dholka is 35 km to the west of Ahmadabad City. According to P.T. Joseph, Dholka revival had begun in April 5, 1905, few months before the Mukti revival. However, according to George, Dholka experienced the revival in 1906.[33] Joseph contents that the living links to this revival are Elambhai Master (alias Elambhai Christian) in Dholka, a grand

---

[29] Helen S. Dyer, (comp.), *Revival in India, 1905-1906* (Akola, Maharashtra: Alliance Publications, 1987), 37-49.

[30] Anderson, *Spreading Fires*, 83.

[31] Bergunder, *The South Indian Pentecostal Movement in the Twentieth Century*, 24.

[32] George, *Trailblazers for God*, 34.

[33] George, *Trailblazers for God*, 34; Wesley Duewel, *Revival Fire* (Michigan: Zondervan Publishing House, 1995), 223.

old man of 83 years, and Rev. B.B. Christian, (Alliance Mission, Maninagar, Ahmedabad), son of V.B. Christian. This revival took place during the lifetime of Elambhai's father Punjabhai Nathubhai.[34] The revival was started in Alliance Church of Dholka. Alliance Missionaries came to Dholka in 1896. They rented a school named Hassanally High School and constructed hostel buildings. In 1900 there was a severe famine. The Alliance missionaries brought 600 orphan boys into the hostel which had been constructed there and the Kheda camp which was another orphanage for girls accommodating about 400 orphans. The revival was started in Bethel Alliance Church of Dholka in a prayer group. Confession of sins and cries of penitence, tongues-speaking and spontaneous prayer meetings even at midnight, were some of the significant manifestations of this revival. The greatest impact of this revival was that a wave of evangelism surged to the surrounding villages.[35] According to Joseph, some believers who received Holy Spirit baptism in April 1905 in Dholka went to the Mukti Mission Ashram of Pandita Ramabai and through them the fire of revival was kindled in Mukti Mission in June 1905.[36]

Miss Sarah Cox, a member of the Christian Missionary Alliance said, 'One after another we missionaries and our Indian Christians were baptised according Acts. 2:4 – many of our small girls,...a number of young men and missionaries received this precious baptism at that time.'[37] Robin Boyd who wrote the church history of Gujarat gives only a faint allusion to this revival and a casual reading may not reveal the fact. He says, 'At times there were among these orphans real experiences of spiritual revival.'[38] It seems mainline

---

[34] P.T. Joseph is a retired advocate of Gujarat high court and actively involved in legal issues related to the Christians in north-India. He has personally visited Elambhai Master in first week of January 2003 and collected the stories of this revival. Elambhai is running a magazine called "Dhumati Sagdi" (Smoking Furnace) in Gujarati language.

[35] Orr, *Evangelical Awakening in South Asia*, 148.

[36] P.T. Joseph, sent the article through mail.

[37] Quoted in George, *Trailblazers for God*, 34.

[38] See Robin Boyd, *Church History of Gujarat* (Madras: The Christian Literature Society, 1981), 110.

historians are not bothered about revivals. Nerius Dholakia, who lives in Ahmedabad, in his work –"Alliance Mission" – has described the 1905 revival in Dholka.[39] It is difficult to ascertain the effect of this revival in the formation of Pentecostal movement in Gujarat.

Revival in Sialkot

Earlier in Punjab the missionaries targeted high caste people and from 1834 to 1885, they had only 447 converts. The American missionary John Hyde was working in Sialkot at the headquarters of the United Presbyterian Mission. He was engaged in constant and extensive prayer for revival and subsequently became known as 'Praying Hyde,' 'the Apostle of Prayer' and 'the man who never sleeps.' The revival broke out early in 1904 in the girl's school at Sialkot in Punjab (now in Pakistan), headed by Mary Campbell, and from there spread to the nearby theological seminary. According to Basil Miller, public confession of sins, holy laughter, dance, clapping of hands, shouting, falling to the ground, trance-like states, and visions of heaven, angels and Jesus were some of the major visible manifestations of this revival.[40]

In the latter days of August 1905, in the second annual convention also the revival continued. Of 300 people gathered most of them were Indian workers, men and women of Punjabi dalit community, but there were also a number of western missionaries from the Scottish and American Presbyterian Missions present. After these revivals the church membership began to increase exponentially. The number of baptised members which stood 3,450 in 1906 became 16,025 by 1915, average annual increase of 1,250. 'This revival, prepared for seven years by Praying Hyde's Punjab Prayer Union, was a classic revival, with conviction and confession of sin and unusual conversions,' comments Edwin Orr.[41] This revival spread

---

[39] Nerius Peter Dholakia, "A Survey and Critical Evaluation of the Christian and Missionary Alliance Ministries in Gujarat," M.Th. thesis, South Asia Institute of Advanced Christian Studies, 1990.

[40] Basil Miller, *Praying Hyde: The Story of John Hyde, A Man of Prayer* (Belfast, Northern Ireland: Ambassador, 2000), 47.

[41] J. Edwin Orr, The Outpouring of the Spirit in Revival and Awakening and its Issue in Church Growth (British Church Growth Association, 2000; http://

into different parts of Punjab as well as into state of Uttar Pradesh, places like Dehra Dun, Almora, Moradabad and Allahabad.[42]

However, according to James Massey, it was a Punjabi Dalit Christian, named Ditt,[43] played major role in the revival and conversion movement. J. Waskom Pickett in his famous book, 'Christian Mass Movements in India' commented the real founder of the church in Sialkot as 'not Gordon, but Ditt.'[44] He brought more than 500 people from his caste into the faith in the 11 years of his baptism (1884). By 1915, almost all the dalits known as *churas* of Sialkot became Christians.[45] It seems that the real hero of this movement was left out by many of the historians. Today many of the Punjabi dalits both Christians and non-Christians are turning to Pentecostal movement.

Revival at Calcutta

The arrival of Alfred Garr and Lillian Garr, the first missionaries from Azusa Street revival, in late December 1906 prepared a ground for Pentecostal revival in Calcutta and nearby regions. Garr was invited to speak in Women's Union Missionary Society (WMUS) and some of the missionaries experienced the visitation of the Spirit.[46] At the invitation of Pastor C.H. Hook, January 13, 1907 Garr began to conduct services at the Carey Baptist Chapel in Lal Bazaar in Calcutta, which was built by William Carey. It was the time of missionary conference and missionaries had come from across

www.churchmodel.org.uk/Orr%20HS% 20BOOKLET%20 A4.pdf (accessed 12 January 2010); Also see Basil Miller, *Praying Hide: A Man of Prayer* (Michigan: Zondervan Publishing House, 1943).

[42] Duewel, *Revival Fire*, 223-227.

[43] For a brief sketch of the story of Ditt see Massey, "Christianity among the Dalits in North India with Special Reference to Punjab," 10-11.

[44] J. Waskom Pickett, *Christian Mass Movements in India* (New York: Abingdon Press, 1933), 56.

[45] Pickett, *Christian Mass Movements in India,* 47-49; Also see John C.B. Webster, *The Christian Community and Change in Nineteenth Century North India* (Delhi: Macmillan, 1976), 231.

[46] Gary B. McGee, "The Calcutta Revival of 1907 and the Reformulation of Charles Parham's Bible Evidence Doctrine." *AJPS* 6, no. 1 (2003): 123.

the subcontinent and Ceylon (now Sri Lanka). With the ministry of Garr a deep sense of conviction of sin resulted in repentance and also praising God in top of the voices. McGee observes that under the inspiration of the Spirit, people began to sing in 'tongues' in unison, even glossographia and intercessory prayers with 'groans that word cannot express' (Rom. 8:26).[47] The revival manifestations included a deep sense of conviction of sin, public confession of sin, falling to the floor, howling, shrieking, groaning, praising and holy laughter.[48] Many of the foreign missionaries from denominational churches experienced baptism in the Holy Spirit and spoke in tongues.[49]

As a continuation of the revival another move of the Spirit broke out in Calcutta in the ministry of Alfred and Josephine Garr in 1907 in the Elliot Road orphanage run by Miss Fannie Simpson a Methodist missionary. Many of the girls in the orphanage were baptised in the Holy Spirit. Miss Simpson also experienced the baptism of Holy Spirit, which created tension between her and the leadership and eventually she was called back to USA. However, later she returned to India as an independent Pentecostal missionary and established a girl's orphanage in Purulia about 1915.[50]

What is significant in these revivals is that even though western missionaries involved in revival across north India, the leaders of the revivals were almost always Indian people themselves. The only exception is the Calcutta revival where a foreign missionary was in the forefront. Further, following each revival a large number of people joined the churches.[51] However, these were not Pentecostal churches but the existing missionary churches. For example, according to Wesley Duewel, the number of Christians in Punjab quadrupled from 37,695 to 163,994.[52] These revivals had prepared the ground for Pentecostal mission activities in successive decades. Here we shall

---

[47] McGee, "The Calcutta Revival of 1907 and the Reformulation of Charles Parham's Bible Evidence Doctrine," 124.

[48] McGee, "Calcutta Revival," 128-29.

[49] McGee, "Pentecostal Phenomena and Revivals in India," 121.

[50] A.C. George, *Trailblazers for God: A History of Assemblies of God in India* (Bangalore: SABC, 2004), 35.

[51] Duewel, *Revival Fire,* 227.

[52] Duewel, *Revival Fire,* 227.

concentrate the Pentecostal mission and subsequent church growth until 1920 in north India.

Early North Indian Pentecostal Mission (1906-1920)

As already pointed out, the Pentecostal history in India is essentially the Pentecostal mission proceeded after the revivals. The revivals were not end in themselves but led to widespread mission campaigns in most part of India. It is interesting to see that these revivals generated passion for evangelism and mission. Additionally, they had such a tremendous effect upon the believers that without any external support they began to spread the message of the gospel to the un-reached. Here we shall not look into the Pentecostal missionary activities took place in four south India states as it is already documented. Similarly, the history of Pentecostalism in Northeast India has been also briefly documented and therefore we do not have to discuss here.[53] Instead, our methodology here is to concentrate on the history of those locations and eras of north India that are not yet unravelled.[54] However, it is also significant to seek to have a glimpse of the missionary endeavours ensued after the revivals events in north India which may give us continuity in pursuing the later part of the history.

Mission in North India

The Mukti-Revivals in north India had far reaching effects not only in India but also in international level.[55] The news of Mukti-Revival stirred similar revivals in Valparaiso and Santiago in Chile, South America in 1909. According to Anderson, the Chilean Pentecostalism has its roots in Mukti-Revival and which did not promote a doctrine of 'initial evidence.'[56]

---

[53] O. L. Snaitang (ed.), *Churches of Indigenous Origin in Northeast India* (Delhi: ISPCK, 2000); There are several articles about the indigenous churches formed due to the revivals in northeast India in this edited work; and also see Snaitang, "The Indigenous Pentecostal Movement in Northeast India," 5-11.

[54] The only exception is the Pentecostal history of Rajasthan documented by Wessly Lukose.

[55] Anderson, *Spreading Fires*, 87.

[56] Anderson, *Spreading Fires*, 89.

The Mukti Revival lasted for a year and a half and resulted in 1100 baptisms at the school. More than 700 of these young women as teams ventured into the surrounding areas with the gospel message sometimes even for more than a month and about 100 of them going out daily even suffering persecution.[57] Thus, the Mukti operated as the main centre in India for Pentecostalism and many from different places received Spirit-baptism and spread the fire in their respective places.[58] The Mukti girls travelled to different places in Maharashtra like, Bombay, Yeotmal, Pune, Ratnagiri, Hoshangabad, Aurangabad and many places and wherever they went the revival fire touched those entire places.[59] J. Edwin Orr in his history of the Evangelical awakening describes the spread of the revival through the Mukti bands that carried the message throughout the Maratha country.[60] The spiritual movement spread across various denominations like Alliance, Anglican, Baptist, Friends, Methodist, Presbyterian, etc. Moreover, the Dhond mission started by Albert Norton, which was near to Kedgaon, also experienced the revival and became a mission centre for North India and he termed it as "one of the mother colonies for Pentecostal work in India."[61] The saddest part, however, is that we do not have the details of the works they carried out and the places they have reached.[62]

One of the most significant mission activities were related to famine relief and empowering the marginalised and oppressed in the society.[63] The women were at the forefront of the mission activities, which had a profound effect upon the status of women in the

---

[57] Anderson, *Spreading Fires*, 79, 86 and 87. Ramabhai also formed a 'Bible School' of 200 young women for prayer and evangelism and they spread the revival fire wherever they went.

[58] Anderson, *Spreading Fires*, 87.

[59] Duewel, *Revival Fire*, 222-223.

[60] J. Edwin Orr, *Evangelical Awakenings in India* (New Delhi: Masihi Sahitya Sanstha, 1970), 111-14.

[61] Anderson, *Spreading Fires*, 86.

[62] It seems that people from there moved to different states of north-India such as Uttar Pradesh, Rajasthan and spread the Pentecostal message, however, those activities had not documented.

[63] Anderson, *Spreading Fires*, 86-88.

context of the low status and oppression of women. Moreover, there was openness to other Christians, "an ecumenicity and inclusiveness that stand in stark contrast to the rigid exclusivism of subsequent Pentecostal movements."[64] Yet, ironically, the Mukti Revival did not contribute in terms of Pentecostal church growth and even after 100 years, Pentecostal works are scant in those parts of Maharashtra. There can be various reasons, such as hard socio-religious context as well as lack of strong and enduring leadership. Most of them were illiterate women who were in the fore-front of the evangelistic activities and in a patriarchal and caste-ridden society like India, that era would not have given enough space to thrive the movement.

Mission in Calcutta and Surrounding Places

The Garrs began to spread the Pentecostal message different part of India and Srilanka and Hong Kong. Their strategy was to reach the existing missionaries, who knew local languages and customs, so that they may later spread the Pentecostal fire. This resulted in the formation of Pentecostal networks and spreading of Pentecostalism in rapid pace.[65] Many who received Pentecostal experience or were thrown out from their parental mission bodies began to develop their own Pentecostal mission. These independent missionaries purchased properties and opened mission stations in larger cities along the railroad lines to facilitate evangelism. However, north India proved to be hardest mission field and missionaries could not make considerable foray into cast-ridden and superstitious minds of the people.[66] Then, the early Pentecostal missionaries concentrated on establishing institutions such as orphanages, elementary and industrial schools, correspondence schools, radio programmes, leper asylums and dispensaries.[67]

---

[64] Anderson, *Spreading Fires*, 88.

[65] Anderson, *Spreading Fires*, 90.

[66] McGee, "Pentecostal Phenomena and Revivals in India," 124.

[67] McGee, "Pentecostal Phenomena and Revivals in India," 124. The AG has the most extensive system of institutional networks such as an orphanage and girl's school at Bettiah; a girl's orphanage at Purilia; the James Harwey Boys' school at Nawabganj; a leper work at Uska Bazar, begun in 1911 by Minnie Abrams; the "Baby Fold" at Rupaidiha; a girl's industrial school at Siswa Bazar, etc., the best

A revival broke out in the school and orphanage run by Shorat Chakrabarty, a Bengali woman with an MA degree who founded Pentecostal mission in Allahabad with her co-worker Dorothea Chandra in 1910. This place became a centre for the spread of Pentecostalism and many were converted and baptised in the Spirit here.[68] Faizabad, Bahraich and Basti near Nepal became main centres of Pentecostalism and buzzing mission activities had occurred. During 1910, there was significant Pentecostal expansion all over Punjab and North-West India. In 1911, mission stations were established in Basti district nearing Nepal by Robert Massey,[69] Dick Mahaffey and Minnie Abrams. A number of 'All India Pentecostal Conferences' were held in different places and they acted as catalyst in Pentecostal mission and growth in different regions of north India and Nepal.[70] Allan Anderson describes many anonymous missionaries in Nepal and surrounding places and even two Indian missionaries going to Iraq whose fate is unknown. Similarly, many Indian evangelists laboured sacrificially to spread the Pentecostal message. For instance, a Brahmin couple, a Dr. and Mrs Kumode Goswami were converted and joined Pentecostal mission, went along with Robert Massey and entered into Nepal to distribute Gospel every day.[71]

Many missionaries of conservative mission societies received spirit-baptism and they were familiar with Indian languages. By 1913, some 200 of these foreign missionaries began to spread Pentecostal message. Similar stories of missionary accomplishments are available to us. In Punch, a part of Kashmir two Anglo-Indian

---

known AG work is in Calcutta, "Mission of Mercy" which now feeds over 20,000 hungry people every day, a hospital, a school of nursing, a junior college, a vocational school, six village clinics, a hostel for destitute youth, a drug prevention program, and 12 schools that provide instruction for 6,000 children. Also see Burgess, 'Pentecostalism in India, 92-93.

[68] Anderson, *Spreading Fires*, 90. In 1911, Chakrabarty moved her centre to Nanpara in the northern Bahraich District and organised a Pentecostal convention in which many missionaries received Spirit-baptism.

[69] This mission was taken over by James Harvey and joined with AG in 1916 and established an orphanage, home for widows, and training school for boys. See Anderson, *Spreading Fires*, 93.

[70] Anderson, *Spreading Fires*, 91-92.

[71] Anderson, *Spreading Fires*, 92.

women, Edith Kirschner and L.A. Baker worked since 1910 under much hardship, ran a girl's schools and converted some Muslims, which resulted in physical violence against them. A revival broke out in 1919-20 in Quaker mission in Itarsi, in Madhya Pradesh, which was led by Indians such as Khushi Lal, Jaganath, Pyare Lal and Har Chand and spread to several other Quaker missions.[72]

Similarly, Maud Orlebar, CMA Missionary opened a 'Pentecostal home' (Beulah Home) for tarrying for Spirit-baptism in Bombay in 1908, became a centre for Pentecostalism where Indian evangelists, Bible women were trained. People from Dalit and tribal communities were accommodated, ran a school for their children and a refuge for women. Vibrant mission activities occurred through native workers, especially Gumut Row, who started a first Pentecostal paper in an Indian language, Marathi. Later Annie Murray began a work in Aurangabad among the poor, where many becoming Pentecostal believers through the work of four Indian preachers with their own expenses.[73]

The Pentecostal denomination which had its presence in north India from the earliest days of Pentecostal movement was the Assemblies of God (AoG). The missionaries of AoG worked in different pockets of various states as early as 1910. However, they could not make much impact until 1970 and the churches planted were few in numbers. We may not discuss its history here as A.C. George gives a detailed account of the north Indian history of AoG from the beginning.[74]

Here it is almost impossible to retell all the stories of early Pentecostal mission. Anderson has collected missionary letters and other available sources to present a fairly complete picture until 1920. Now what is unknown is the story of Pentecostal mission from 1920 to 1960. We will make some efforts to glance into those years even though it may be difficult to find credible eye witnesses who know all those 40 years of happenings. However, before that we will analyse the early Pentecostal mission to know what traits it had possessed.

[72] Anderson, *Spreading Fires*, 92.

[73] Anderson, *Spreading Fires*, 93-94.

[74] A.C. George, *Trailblazers for God: A History of Assemblies of God in India* (Bangalore: SABC, 2004).

The above study shows that the early Pentecostal mission had certain Indian peculiarities, which can give clues for further expansion of mission today. The most significant aspect of the Pentecostal mission was its indigenous and contextual nature from its inception.[75] The Indian situation was unlike western and needed different approaches. As Paulson argues, the concept of faith ministry and the Indian freedom movement sensitised many to chart an Indian course and assert independence from foreign mission control to carry out the mission by faith according to the contextual needs.[76]

As already seen the major part of the missionary endeavours were organised and executed by native evangelists, the common believers, who had burning passion for evangelism owing to their Spirit-baptism, though their names and contributions are largely forgotten as western missionaries did not mention them in their correspondence.[77] Moreover, Western missionaries had the disadvantage of language, geography, culture and hot climate in India. The native leaders from existing Christian communities took the leadership roles in mission. Indian freedom struggle also contributed to the emergence of native leadership.[78] Women were at the forefront

---

[75] Ramabhai's words underline the fact: Let the revival come to Indians so as to suit their nature and feelings [as] God has made them. He knows their nature, and He will work out His purpose in them in a way which may not conform with the ways of western people and their lifelong training...The first report of the revival in India entitled "Pentecost in India" was carried in the third issue of *The Apostolic Faith* in Los Angeles is Quoted by Allan Anderson says: News comes from India that the baptism with the Holy Ghost and gift of tongues is being received there by natives who are simply taught of God. See Anderson, *Spreading Fires*, 75 and 80.

There are abundant testimonies regarding indigenous and contextual aspects of Indian Pentecostalism, see P.J. Titus, "Pentecostal indigenous Movements in Andhra;" Siga Arles, "Indigenous Church Growth at Kolar;" Paul C. Martin, "The Ceylon Pentecostal Mission;" Sara Abraham, 'The Indian Pentecostal Church of God and its Indigenous Nature;" in *Christianity is Indian: The Emergence of an Indigenous Community*, rev. ed. Edited by Roger E. Hedlund (Delhi: ISPCK, 2004).

[76] Pulikottil, "Emergence of Indian Pentecostalism," 54-56, and Bergunder, "Constructing Indian Pentecostalism," 199-200.

[77] Anderson, "Revising Pentecostal History in Global Perspective."

[78] Pulikottil, "Emergence of Indian Pentecostalism," 52-56.

of mission, especially in north Indian context.[79] The Spirit-filled women – western or Indian – became powerful instruments in the hands of God to liberate many. There were no ecclesiastical clutches to stop them from exercising the Spirit-given freedom in mission. Many powerful women leaders stand in the row with great exploits in the Indian mission scenario. At the same time, the Western Pentecostal missionaries had also contributed enormously to the growth of the mission by giving leadership, Biblical teaching and financial assistance. They have forfeited all comforts to labour in a hard-land and at any cost Indian mission history cannot forget their heroic lives.

Another salient feature of the Indian mission was its emphasis on social aspect of mission, especially in north India. Missionaries had established many institutions, which serve the society even today. The poor and the destitute were cared for and education and healthcare were offered. Another remarkable aspect of the mission was its emphasis on miraculous aspects of the work of the Spirit. It was not merely the missionary efforts, but missionaries were conscious of their limitations and emphasised the gifts of the Spirit such as healing, prophecy, exorcism etc. Therefore, the mission was effective beyond the handicap of language, culture, education or oratory skills.

It is clear that the Pentecostal movement in India was the result of the great revivals occurred in different places and various times. In a landscape of spiritual dryness and stagnation, these revivals came as a downpour to revive the churches and society. They created a space for the Pentecostal movement to take its roots in both hostile social as well as spiritual context. The Indian societies at those times were not conducive enough to absorb the Pentecostal message. Moreover, the ecclesiastical structures were not open for a drastic change in doctrines and practices. The Spirit manifestations were either considered as lunatic behaviour or evil spirit infestations. The Spirit-

---

[79] Though south India had some women workers, may be due to ecclesiastical traditions there were not many leaders arose. However, we should not forget the fact that even today women are the significant force behind the Indian Pentecostal mission; see Michael Bergunder, "Women and Leadership in the South Indian Pentecostal Movement," *Dharma Deepika 6/2* (July-December 2002): 35-40.

filled people were being watched with suspicion and not welcomed in the historic churches. Those who received the Spirit visitations were mainly the poor, dalits or women who neither had social standing, financial resources nor educational qualifications. Yet, the movement began to grow into hard terrains of north India even though it could not make an impact similar to the south Indian movement.

Chapter 5

North Indian Pentecostal History (1920-1960)

This period can be rightly termed as a transition period in Pentecostal movement in north India and is plagued by a dearth of documented historical resources. It may also be rightly called as 'the dark era of the north Indian Pentecostal movement and history' or what we can call 'cooling off' period of the movement with most missing links of the north Indian Pentecostal history. It is hard to dig out every possible reason behind such a morbid state and the decline of the movement.

At the same time the south Indian Pentecostalism was moving forward and increasing in number of congregations and in mission activities. As we look into this period of the north Indian Pentecostal history we need to take great caution not to jump into conclusions but study the context of that era and search into all available resources. It is also significant to have a comparative study of the south Indian Pentecostalism, especially the Kerala Pentecostalism with north India to see what factors were caused to the decline of the movement. We need to tread this area very cautiously as none has ever travelled before. As Anderson says we shall approach this era 'reading between the lines.'[1] To have a better picture we shall explore both internal and external factors that played negative roles in dampening the enthusiasm of the movement and resultant 'cooling off' effect.

1 Anderson, "Revising Pentecostal History in Global Perspective," 158-165.

Departure of Foreign Pentecostal Missionaries: Even though the revivals had wide-ranging impact, the mission followed was not sustained in long run in north India, especially in the case of the Mukti revival. There can be many reasons[2] but the immediate one is the lack of strong leadership who would consolidate the movement into church growth. After 1920, many of the foreign Pentecostal missionaries went back to their own native places as they were getting old and some of them were already dead. The reason behind this assumption is, many of the Pentecostal missionaries were already serving in India for several years in other missionary churches and the experience of Spirit-baptism led them to be Pentecostal missionaries. For instance, Alfred Garr targeted already existing missionaries who knew the local languages and customs (as expected he could not speak the Indian languages with the gift of tongues). Anderson says, 'The focus of their ministry was now on reaching missionaries with their message...because these missionaries (unlike the Garrs) knew the customs and languages of India...Most of these came from evangelical faith missions like the CMA and the CIM, but sometimes missionaries from older denominations were affected.'[3] Burgess also says that about sixty veteran missionaries living in India embraced the Pentecostal gift of tongues.[4]

Besides, the heat of Indian freedom movement began increasingly felt upon foreign missionaries in this era. The foreign missionaries were in the control of administration as well as financial matters and as we know the missionaries did not involve native missionaries in administration or finance.[5] This might have led to a paralysis of administrative and mission activities. As foreign missionaries left, the existing mission activities had experienced financial crunch which could have played as a major constraining factor in the growth and consolidation of the movement.

---

[2] The North-Indian situation was not favorable for mission with its rigid caste-system, strong cultural and religious binding, and lack of Christian exposure to the general population. Christianity was considered as a foreign religion and despised as religion of meat-eaters.

[3] Anderson, *Spreading Fires*, 90.

[4] Burgess, "Pentecostalism in India," 89.

[5] Anderson, "Revising Pentecostal History in Global Perspective," 163-164.

Moreover, in north India the people converted were mostly from poor and lower caste background and missionaries were helping them financially and many new converts were staying in 'mission compounds.' The missionaries patronised the native converts and kept them in the safety of mission compound. Even in Pentecostal missions this way of missionary paternalism was widely practised.[6] Benjamin P. Shinde[7] argued that mission station model retarded the development of Indian Pentecostal leadership in the North.[8] Thus, the departure of foreign missionaries probably dampened the enthusiasm as well as the financial resources of common believers. This would have led to the 'cooling off' the movement.

However, in the south, especially in Kerala, the most of the native missionary leaders were from Syrian Christian background and began 'faith ministry' and harnessed their own resources. As mission began to grow, they walked away from missionary paternalism and asserted their independence and launched their own church movements. Pulikottil in this regard comments that native leadership with a considerable following had been developed in Kerala and they took the Pentecostal faith to the rest of South India and were the founding fathers of the Pentecostal Faith in Tamil Nadu, Andhra Pradesh, and parts of Karnataka.[9]

Non-Formation of Pentecostal Congregations: Yet another significant factor that led to the decline of the Pentecostal movement in the north was the lack of strong native Pentecostal churches. We do not exactly know the number of Pentecostal congregations began with the revival movements. For example, even though the Mukti revival was so powerful, it is not apparent whether any

---

[6] Anderson, "Revising Pentecostal History in Global Perspective," 159.

[7] Benjamin P. Shinde was a product of the Junnar Boy's Orphanage and one of the earliest trained Indian missiologists; B. Shinde, "The Contribution of the Assemblies of God to Church Growth in India" (M.A. thesis, Fuller Theological Seminary, School of World Mission, 1974).

[8] Burgess, "Pentecostalism in India," 93.

[9] Paulson Pulikottil, "Emergence of Indian Pentecostalism," *Dharma Deepika* (July-December 2002), 52-55. For example, Indian Pentecostal Church, an independent church movement by K.E. Abraham and other co-workers in Kerala.

Pentecostal congregations were formed by the Mukti missionaries.[10] The spiritual and the missionary activities were all taken place in the existing churches. It seems that most of the people who were revived remained in their own existing denominations. Further, some of the great Christians of those times like Sadhu Sundhar Singh were against the formation of ecclesiological structures. However, in the south people who were part of the revivals formed independent Pentecostal congregations, later organised into major Pentecostal denominations.[11] Unlike south India, a strong church growth movement did not attain in the north. Missionaries were primarily concentrated on running orphanages, rescue homes for widows, schools etc.[12]

Lack of Native Leadership: Although, the revivals had wide-ranging impact, the mission followed was not sustained in long-run in north India. The immediate reason is the lack of strong native leadership who would consolidate the movement into church growth. Most of the converts were uneducated and from dalit or lower-caste setting and they were not trained to lead in the fore-front. They were always in supportive roles. Foreign missionaries did not ordain any native leaders until 1930.[13] Besides because of intense opposition, missionaries in North India often set up mission stations with a church, school, and missionary residence. As mentioned earlier, such mission station model retarded the development of Indian Christian leadership in the North.[14] However, in Kerala by the second decade of the twentieth century, a second line of local leaders were beginning

---

[10] Allan Anderson, *An Introduction to Pentecostalism* (Cambridge: Cambridge University Press, 2004), 124; Anderson, *Spreading Fires*, 88 and Bergunder, *The South Indian Pentecostal Movement in the Twentieth Century*, 24; J. Edwin Orr, *Evangelical Awakenings in Southern Asia* (Minneapolis: Bethany Fellowship, 1975).

[11] K. E. Abraham, *Yesukristhuvinte Eliya Dassan* [Autobiography of Pastor K.E. Abraham]. 3rd ed. (Kumbanad, India: K.E. Abraham Foundation, 2001); Mathew, *Kerala Penthecosthu Charithram.*

[12] Gary B. McGee & S. M. Burgess, "India." *The New International Dictionary of Pentecostal and Charismatic Movements* (Michigan: Zondervan Publishing House, 2002): 124.

[13] Paulson Pulikottil, "Emergence of Indian Pentecostalism," *Dharma Deepika* (July-December 2002), 52.

[14] Burgess, "Pentecostalism in India," 93.

to challenge foreign missionary leadership monopoly.[15] By 1930, native leadership became strong with a considerable following and established churches all over south India.[16] Therefore, it is safe to assume that the local leadership was not strong enough to carry out further church growth activities as foreign missionaries seldom considered native missionaries at par with them.

Lack of Theological and Missionary Training: Even though early Pentecostals had their mission in the power of the Spirit and achieved considerable results, they failed to develop indigenous means and methods to articulate their own theology according to the contextual needs. The foreign missionaries were neither theologically trained nor had the ability and flexibility to form a contextual spirituality. Many of them were trained in the denominational set-up and even after the Spirit-experience, their theology remained same except in few areas such as the doctrine of tongue-speaking or Spirit-baptism. Of course, we are not discounting the formation of the "four-fold gospel" and other doctrines.[17] These were suitable for south India, especially Kerala, as it had considerable Christian population. However, the north Indian mission context needed much more innovation due to unfavorable conditions such as rigid caste-system, strong cultural and religious binding, and lack of Christian exposure to the general population. Christianity was considered as a foreign religion and despised as religion of meat-eaters.

The biblical and missionary training essential to endure the movement was not available at that era, because the mission proceeded immediately after the revivals were so hectic. The local missionaries as well as believers were not given with solid biblical teaching to continue the Pentecostal life style and evangelism; instead foreign missionaries might have used their help to further expand the mission. Moreover, early Pentecostal missionaries lacked an adequate theology of mission. Instead, Pentecostals relied on the same old western methods which were used among Christian population in the west, which acted as detrimental to the growth of mission. This

---

[15] Hedlund, "Critique of Pentecostal Mission by a Friendly Evangelical," 82.

[16] Pulikottil, "Emergence of Indian Pentecostalism," 53.

[17] The fourfold Gospel or full Gospel is the fourfold devotion to Jesus Christ as the Saviour, Spirit Baptiser, Healer and Coming King.

anomaly has reflected in the subsequent years and Indian missionaries faced many major roadblocks in pioneering missions.[18] Even today, the pioneering missionaries from Kerala Pentecostalism in north India face same situation.

Schisms: Mission was carried out by people and organisations having no long term vision or corporate-spirit, what is typically 'Pentecostal.' Lack of co-ordination among the leaders and division dodged the progress. Personal prejudice, organisational envy, theological dogmatism and cultural-superiority and many other factors hampered the unity of mission and had negative effects. As a result, within few years of its inception, Pentecostal movement had split into many western and Indian organisations. Therefore, their efforts were not produced the intended fruits.

The Indian Pentecostal mission lacked the ecumenical-spirit and formed ghetto-mentality and had no fellowship with other denominations as well as among themselves. Pentecostals thus, lost the opportunity to evangelise the society, instead spend their energy and time in wrangling and backbiting. Lack of women leadership also can be a reason for its dwindling state. Although, women were in the vanguard of Indian mission, many were unable to come to the leadership position except a few.[19] The possible reasons were like, opposition from culture, society, ecclesiastical structure and so on. However, this has snatched the prospect of attracting women of Indian context most of them under crushing poverty and patriarchal oppression. Further, Pentecostals did not show any interest in social involvement. In a caste-ridden society where most of the people undergo severe caste-oppression and economic hardship, the Pentecostal mission was so engrossed in saving the souls that it grossly missed opportunity to formulate a systematic involvement in society and opposing the evil practices such as the cast-system and other oppressive structures of Indian society. Even inside the church discrimination was rampant and continues even today.[20]

---

[18] Reuben Louis Gabriel, "Reflections on Indian Pentecostalism: Trends and Issues," *Dharma Deepika* 6/2 (July-December 2002): 69-71.

[19] Michael Bergunder, "Women and Leadership," 35.

[20] Samuel Kutty, *The Place and Contribution of Dalits,* 134-140.

Socio-Political Context: The period subsequent to 1920 was one of the turbulent eras of Indian society. The political discontent against the British rule was its zenith. There were many movements against the colonial rule and oppression such as 'Non-cooperation movement, 'Self-rule movement' (*swaraj*) 'Quit India Movement,' etc. Even though Christian missionaries were against the enslavement and exploitation of the native people, general population, especially in the north considered Christianity as the religion of the oppressors. There was a general animosity against Christianity in the north and the political nationalism of Hindutva forces was utterly against Christian missionaries. This political climate definitely affected the growth of the movement.

Religio-Cultural Context: As already mentioned, the religio-cultural context of north India acted as a formidable factor in the non-proliferation of Pentecostalism in north India. North-Indian Hindu society was an impervious target unlike south Indian Christian society. General population did not know what Christianity was and considered it as a pagan religion. Indeed the educational and charitable activities were appreciated by a section of the society; however, the conversion was a contentious issue. Moreover, the cast-ridden north India divided itself into various groups and sub-groups and some considered Christianity as the religion of dalits and lower-castes as most of the converts from those backgrounds. The patriarchal and andro-centric society acted as a rigid structure for the first missionaries, mostly women.

Suppression of the Work of the Spirit by Missionary Churches: Another possible reason for the lack of growth of Pentecostal movement in the north might be the suppression of the work of the Spirit by denominational churches. As already noted many of the people who received the baptism of the Spirit remained in their respective churches. Many missionaries or pastors who were from the denominational background could not digest the manifestations of the Spirit such as tongue-speaking, shaking of the body and other signs and considered them as demonic. At least some of them were influenced by the Western Enlightenment thinking and western liberal theology that relegated the supernatural. The believers who experienced the work of the Spirit did not have the essential biblical knowledge to defend their experience since most of them were illiterate or had only partial knowledge in the biblical teaching. This might have dampened the initial enthusiasm and prevented the believers from exercising the gifts of the Spirit regularly and witnessing in the society.

Coming of Kerala Pentecostal Missionaries

The general spiritual climate of denominational churches was in decline in this era. Many of the Pastors were not concerned about the spiritual growth of their parishioners and people spend their life as name-sake Christians. Even if any pastors or believers showed any spiritual inclination such as praying in loud voice, tongue speaking etc., the higher church officials would discourage it. The Christians who lived in the mission compounds were name-sake Christians and some of them were even drunkards. Even today, at least in some places the so called 'mission compound' Christians are infamous for their evil and immoral habits.

Even though above mentioned factors acted as detrimental to the proliferation of the Pentecostal churches in the north, many believers who experienced the Spirit-baptism and revival continued to keep the experience intact and kept the revival fire burning in personal life. This assumption is proved right because when Kerala Pentecostal missionaries reached in north India, it was these Spirit-filled people or at least those who knew about this experience responded to them. In fact the south Indian missionaries did not approach Hindus first in their mission activities but tried to reach out already who were Christians in denominational churches. Moreover, some of these Christians in north India had a great zeal for evangelism. For example, M.K. Chacko, the first pioneer Pentecostal missionary from Kerala to north India in 1937 was initially sponsored by one Miss Karen Kamath from Bombay, a Swedish missionary who was very zealous and ready to work with native pastors.[21] When Chacko moved to Kanpur, there also a Christian called Masih Das supported him. Later when Chacko left Kanpur to Delhi he entrusted the mission

[21] Chacko, *An Autobiography*, 9-10; Also see Thomas, *God's Trailblazer*, 26.

work in the hands of Miss Kamat and Masih Das.[22] Unfortunately, the details of these people are not given by Chacko. We may assume that they had previous Pentecostal experience and that was why they were ready to join Chacko in his Pentecostal activities and Chacko was ready to handover the work to them. However, Kurien Thomas gives us more details. Miss Kamat later went to Lahore (now in Pakistan) and worked with Pastor K.J. Samuel and continued even after the partition.[23]

After coming to north India, Chacko worked in Kanpur for six months. In Pratapgarh, Rev. Ericsson invited him to conduct meetings in his church and in Mussoorie in U.P. Although Chacko did not mention his church affiliation, most probably he could be from one of the missionary churches. Again, Chacko says that he was invited to speak in a missionary conference in Mahoba in U.P. in 1938 and many people received the baptism of the Holy Spirit. There were opposition from the missionaries except by one Mrs. M`clviei.[24] Therefore, it seems that at least some of the mission organisations were in search of spiritual fervour and ready to allow a person from Pentecostal orientation to preach in their conference.

Then pastor Chacko and his family moved to Delhi. As he testifies in his autobiography, his family suffered poverty and even did not have woollen clothes to be protected from the extreme cold of Delhi. There he was invited by a Delhi Methodist pastor P.D. Philip many times and once Chacko had a week's special meeting in that church and because of this some people began to attend Chacko's church. He also speaks about Delhi Methodist bishop Rev. Bedley who extended 'some help' to him.[25] Again he was invited by Methodist bishop Baker and Rev. Lance to speak in a minister's conference in Roorkee (now in Uttarakhand state). Chacko narrates it this way: 'I preached the full gospel truth. Many pastors and ministers were against me but those who invited me said that what I preached was correct.'[26] Besides he was invited to preach in missionary

[22] Chacko, *An Autobiography,* 13-14.

[23] Thomas, *God's Trailblazer,* 26-27.

[24] Chacko, *An Autobiography,* 12-13.

[25] Chacko, *An Autobiography,* 15.

[26] Chacko, *An Autobiography,* 16.

conferences of Baptist Mission, Swedish mission, Norwegian mission etc., and according to him, he 'went to wherever full gospel was not preached.'[27] What is obvious from these stories is, although there was a general decline of spiritual fervour among the Christians in the north, few people kept the revived spirit and had spiritual longing.

In Delhi through his ministry many people were healed from various sicknesses and also delivered of evil spirits.[28] In Agra, Chacko stayed with Harry Liddle and his effort had seen the formation of a congregation which had handed over to Liddle.[29] Then he moved to Moradabad and established a church. Furthermore, from his discussion of his story it seems that there were some Pentecostal churches existed in 1930's in U.P and surrounding places. He says that in his evangelistic outreach if anybody were converted or any Pentecostal congregations were established, he would entrust new converts in the local church and the church to the local people.[30] As already we have seen and Kurien Thomas also testifies that, Chacko handed over the church he established in Agra to two young men, Harry Liddle and Joni Peters.[31] Indeed, those would be Pentecostal churches. He also mentions about a baptismal service in a Pentecostal church existed in Nawabganj in U.P. led by Pastor Gideon.[32] This could be the AoG church and related James Harvey boys school at Nawabganj.[33] Nonetheless, from his testimony it is almost impossible to decipher out how much Pentecostal works in Delhi and surrounding states existed in 1930's and subsequent decade. Of course, there was no Pentecostal church in Delhi and he claims that his congregation was the first Pentecostal church. He also states that

---

[27] Chacko, *An Autobiography,* 21.

[28] Chacko, *An Autobiography,* 18.

[29] Chacko, *An Autobiography,* 19.

[30] Chacko, *An Autobiography,* 21-22.

31 Thomas, *God's Trailblazer,* 22-23.

[32] Chacko, *An Autobiography,* 22.

[33] See McGee, "Pentecostal Phenomena and Revivals in India," 124. He describes, "The AG has the most extensive system of institutional networks such as an orphanage and girl's school at Bettiah; a girl's orphanage at Purilia; *the James Harwey Boys' school at Nawabganj*; a leper work at Uska Bazar, begun in 1911 by Minnie Abrams," etc.

he had started many pioneering assemblies in different parts of north India and entrusted them to the local workers.[34] But it is sure that there were some Spirit-filled people who had great enthusiasm for evangelism.

Another Pentecostal missionary who moved to north India from Kerala in 1940's was George Thomas Paradheshi, a powerful servant of the Lord. He renounced everything to become a sage, moved to the Sahya mountain ranges, eating fruits and roots. He had a special anointing to cast out evil spirits and many people were delivered and became Pentecostal believers. Once in Andhra Pradesh, he went to meet a college principal but he refused to meet Paradeshi but sent ten rupees with a peon. Having seen the currency, Paradeshi shouted "devil, devil" and threw the money away. Knowing this incident, the principal came out and Paradeshi shared the gospel message to him. The attitude of the principal was totally changed and along with Paradeshi he preached the gospel in nearby villages. Since then he was known as "George Thomas Satyananda Paradhesi."[35]

Through his ministry many "signs and wonders" were taken place in different states of north India and churches were established. In north India, many people came to Pentecostal fold through his ministry and became prominent Pentecostal leaders. In Jhansi, Madhya Pradesh, Tresseler and family, in Kanpur, Hansen, Maxwell George and Alison Joseph became Pentecostal followers. In Lucknow, B.M. Chand and in Agra Harry Liddle and Christy Liddle, who became instrumental in establishing the Doon Bible College in Dehra Doon.[36]

In 1942, Pastor K.J. Samuel from Kerala had arrived in Lahore (Pakistan) where there was a church formed by Chacko. Chacko baptised Mr. & Mrs. Davis and Das and his family earlier. The church was known as 'Lahore Pentecostal Church'. There were many believers in and around Lahore and there were some Pentecostal works even in some villages like Fathipura and Shekhikhadi. Pastor Samuel extended his mission work and conducted Gospel meetings

---

[34] Chacko, *An Autobiography,* 1.

[35] P.S. Samuel, *Christhuvil Oru Samarppitha Jeevitham: An Autobiography* (Raipur, India: The Church of God, Raipur, 2006), 29-30.

[36] Samuel, *Christhuvil Oru Samarppitha Jeevitham,* 30.

in all important cities of today's Pakistan such as Peshawar, Multan and other cities. It is reported that he was a leading a 'faith' life without any financial aid from anybody. Once he was provided with money by strangers just before reaching the ticket window while he was standing in a queue for ticket to travel. He was miraculously protected from rioting and arsons at the time of the partition (1947). All the people of the village where he was staying left because of communal killing and he and his family were alone for few days. Once he was protected from a notorious killer who came impersonated but only took away some of his valuables.

Kurien Thomas, who became a missionary in Itarsi, was stationed in Lahore for a few months and used to reach out to places like Bhatinda and Ferozpur in the Punjab.[37] There he had special meetings in the home of P.D. Benjamin, a ticket inspector on the Railways. Later Benjamin left his job and involved himself in full-time ministry.[38] Benjamin became a powerful instrument in the formation of Pentecostal churches in states like Gujarat and Maharashtra, mainly in the Tribal areas in 1970.

In 1943, Kurien Thomas, another pioneer missionary from Kerala, along with his friend Pastor John, came to the north. According to him, there existed a small Pentecostal church in Parel, Bombay, led by Pastor Lewis; the ministry of Thomas resulted in a spiritual revival there. Similarly, in Jhansi, Paradeshi had a ministry and established a Pentecostal work some years before Kurian Thomas' arrival. As mentioned earlier, Paradeshi had a special anointing in casting out evil spirits, and the public manifestation of such activities resulted in the baptism of many people and in the formation of a Pentecostal church. When Thomas arrived at the scene, Pastor William Rajandram was leading the church.[39]

In 1945, Thomas settled in Itarsi, Madhya Pradesh for mission works, through Chacko who encouraged him to move there. Chacko had already baptised some Christians from the Friend's Mission

---

37 Thomas, *God's Trailblazer,* 25-26; According to Thomas, there were many believers in and around Lahore and there were some Pentecostal works even in some villages like Fathipura and Shekhikhadi.

38 Thomas, *God's Trailblazer,* 26.

39 Thomas, *God's Trailblazer,* 22.

(Quakers), before Thomas arrived in Itarsi.[40] The Friend's Mission had been working in Itarsi and surrounding villages for many years. However, because of financial difficulties, they had stopped going into the villages, when Thomas arrived in the scene. According to him, he had no support from anybody but by faith began to work in those villages where, later churches were formed.[41] He was accompanied and helped by E. Simon, his sister Mary and his mother Mrs. Simon in evangelism in surrounding villages of Itarsi. Thomas and his wife had to suffer poverty, sickness and extreme climatic condition of North India. He testifies that he was being protected by the Lord from perilous situations several times. In a missionary trip to the city of Banswara, Rajasthan, he was conducting meetings in the house of a medical doctor. During the meeting, the doctor's son came running with a sword to attack him. However, according to Thomas, some unseen force stopped the young man from striking him. In another occasion, he was coming from north Bihar; he heard an inner voice compelling him to get out of the train. Recognizing it as the word of the Lord, he refused to travel on it. After a few hours, he got the news that the train derailed and several passengers had been injured.[42] His family was being miraculously provided with food when they went hungry and granted resources in dire needs.[43]

In 1962, he had begun a Bible school, now known as Central India Bible College, training many native missionaries.[44] Moreover, many churches were established and registered as 'Fellowship of Pentecostal Churches of God', in 1966 which now boasts of 1100 churches in North Indian states and includes many native workers.[45] The mission also runs an orphanage, a vocational centre and clinics.[46]

---

[40] Those Christians were Mr. & Mrs. Francis, three young people, Ebenezer Simon, Miss Mary Simon and a young girl; see Thomas, *God's Trailblazer,* 31.

[41] Thomas, *God's Trailblazer,* 32-33.

[42] Thomas, *God's Trailblazer*, 51.

[43] Thomas, *God's Trailblazer*, 54-55.

[44] Thomas, *God's Trailblazer,* 78-82.

[45] Thomas, *God's Trailblazer,* 87-89; also see Hedlund, *Quest for Identity,* 119.

[46] http://centralindia.org/about-us/our-history/ (accessed on 10/07/2014).

Thomas also mentions one of the early Pentecostal churches in Lucknow in U.P. started by Pastor S.M. Chand, where, in 1960, a mega convention was conducted by T.L. Osborn. Many people were healed of their ailments and there was a great movement of the Spirit. However, opposition from Hindu militants was so strong that the convention had to be stopped. Kurien also had conducted revival meetings in Bhopal in M.P. in 1947 immediately after the independence of India. Earlier many places were ruled by Hindu or Muslim kings and it was forbidden to preach publically. He also visited in Kota, Udaipur, and Ajmer in Rajasthan.[47]

Similarly, another Pentecostal pioneer, P.S. Samuel, began mission work in Raipur, Chhattisgarh, in 1948, among the local tribal people. Through him many churches were established.[48] In the initial stage of his north Indian mission, he worked in various villages in Nagpur district such as Kalmeshar, Dhappawada and Savner village and proclaimed the Pentecostal message. Samuel also travelled to Dhond, Akola, Devalali, Manded, Malkapur and other places in Maharashtra and conducted special meetings. He also visited the Mukti mission and preached there to the students.

Through a vision, he came to Raipur. As he claims, he did not know where the place was but located in a map and reached there in 1948. In Raipur, an army officer, Major W.N. Winfred, approached him and asked him to conduct meetings. Through Samuel many took believers' baptism there. In another instant, a Hindu priest (*pujari*) was attracted to the Pentecostal faith and became an evangelist.[49] Before 1948, the Methodist Mission was working in Raipur; however, when there was no desired result, they sold the property and moved to Jagadalpur. However, Samuel though he had to go through severe troubles and opposition, stayed there and began his missionary activities. According to him, he suffered severe poverty; three months he had to sleep in the railway station.[50]

---

[47] Thomas, *God's Trailblazer,* 75-77.

[48] Mathew, *Kerala Penthecosthu Charithram,* 273; H. Wilfred, "In Fond Memory of P.S. Samuel," *Hallelujah* 11/12 (15 June 2006): 6-7.

[49] Samuel, *Christhuvil Oru Samarppitha Jeevitham,* 52.

[50] Samuel, *Christhuvil Oru Samarppitha Jeevitham,* 69.

In the month of July 1950, Samuel took 40 days of fasting. After this, a revival began to occur and he conducted several prayer meetings in Raja Talab, Raipur. One day, five people including Samuel were praying in a house. As Samuel testifies, the fire from heaven came down on the house and the women of neighbourhood came running shouting "fire, fire". One lady testified that a fire came down from the sky and began to burn on the house where the prayer was conducted. When the women looked into the room, they saw a man in dazzling clothes and they realised that he was Jesus Christ.[51]

The revival continued and there were prayers sometimes lasting for 24 hours; day and night people attended the revival meetings. This annoyed some of the Christian leaders. However, many sick people were healed and many were delivered of evil spirits. According to him, some doctors who were running medical dispensaries nearby areas began to oppose him as they were not getting any patients.[52] This revival continued till 1957; people from distant places used to come to the revival meetings.[53] Samuel and his co-workers conducted several revival meetings in all nearby cities and villages such as Basna, Jagadishpur, Saraipali and so on. They also travelled to Madhya Pradesh, Orissa and West Bengal (Kharakhpur and Kolkotta).[54]

In 1952 a revival occurred in Cuttack through Samuel's ministry and many people spoke in other tongues and churches were established. It was in the mission run by the Anderson Indiana Church of God that revival first occurred. The mission had a church, a high school, an orphanage and a hostel. One Miss High was the principal of the school. More than 100 students, teachers and some more people attended the meeting. It is reported that a powerful manifestation of the Holy Spirit occurred and many students and some teachers were baptised in the Spirit and spoke in tongues. In the evening Samuel left the school for another meeting but the children continued to pray and tarry in the presence of the Lord. Then the Spirit moved among the students in a powerful way and the noise was heard all over the place. Hearing the noise some police men reached

---

[51] Samuel, *Christhuvil Oru Samarppitha Jeevitham,* 73.

[52] Samuel, *Christhuvil Oru Samarppitha Jeevitham,* 76.

[53] Samuel, *Christhuvil Oru Samarppitha Jeevitham,* 114.

[54] Samuel, *Christhuvil Oru Samarppitha Jeevitham,* 119-120.

there and threatened students to get out of the place. However, through some children the Spirit revealed the sins of the police men and they fled away from the scene. When the Mission head quarter in Indianapolis heard the news of the revival, they dismissed Miss High, some teachers and the students who experienced the Spirit's anointing. Miss High later joined a Pentecostal church in Bihar and worked there.[55] In 1953, Samuel established a church at Brijraj Nagar in Sambalpur district of Orissa.[56]

Following the revival, through Samuel, as his autobiography says, many signs and wonders were occurred and even a dead person was raised in Raipur. One doctor Frank Rawaani, who first opposed his ministry, received a divine healing and placed a notice board in his two medical dispensaries that sick people would be prayed for. Sometimes he would sent people to Samuel or accompany patients.[57]

In 1957 he was forced to leave Raipur as one of his co-workers occupied the house he was staying and he travelled to place called Ghoom, near Darjeeling. There a lady missionary from Finland was working for years and she was about to leave the place due to lack any response from the native people. Samuel conducted 15 days of meetings there and through a miraculous event many people were baptised and the mission work began to flourish.[58] According to him, he established the first Pentecostal church in Bhilai. Moreover, he established a Pentecostal church in Tejpur in Assam.[59] 1n 1958 he began some churches in Sikkhim. Similarly, in Bhutan, a village known as Chunabhatta became Pentecostal through his work.[60] In Shillong he had begun a strong Pentecostal movement.[61]

In 1963, several Pentecostal meetings were conducted in Balamghir, Orissa and many were confessed their sins and baptised in the Spirit. Some people opposed the meetings but God's power

[55] Samuel, *Christhuvil Oru Samarppitha Jeevitham,* 154-156.

[56] Samuel, *Christhuvil Oru Samarppitha Jeevitham,* 153.

[57] Samuel, *Christhuvil Oru Samarppitha Jeevitham,* 111-113.

[58] Samuel, *Christhuvil Oru Samarppitha Jeevitham,* 125-126.

[59] Samuel, *Christhuvil Oru Samarppitha Jeevitham,* 132-134.

[60] Samuel, *Christhuvil Oru Samarppitha Jeevitham,* 138-139.

[61] Samuel, *Christhuvil Oru Samarppitha Jeevitham,* 144.

touched them and they all fell down on the ground. In 1965 a Bible school was established in Cuttack and later shifted to Balamghir.[62] There were some divisions happened which is mentioned by Samuel; one of his co-workers took away some of the churches in Ranchi, Bihar and established another denomination called "The Pentecostal Church."[63] Through Samuel several churches were established in Jharkhand, Bihar and Orissa and a Bible College in Raipur.

As we turn to neighbouring state Bihar, it is known as the "the graveyard of the missions." After Independence, most of the foreign missionaries had to leave the country and there was no strong indigenous church or leadership to handle the mission activities that were left behind by the foreign missionaries. Except a few cases, almost all the mission activities in Bihar had to be closed down due to lack of a strong indigenous church and leadership. However, some Pentecostal missionaries began to initiate their activities in Bihar. The Assembly of God Mission came to Bihar in 1910.

The first missionary was Johnson from US and he came to Samasthipur and started a Bible School. However, later the Bible School was shifted to Bettiah. Later another missionary F.. Baugh from US reached Saran District in North Bihar. Later they established their mission work in other parts of North Bihar such as Darbhanga and Muryaro in Samathipur District.[64] The main concentration of AoG mission was in Bettiah and there were many women missionaries. Ana Tomeseck, Grace Walter, Mary Wagoler, B.M. Rich, Thelma Tate were some of the single lady missionaries who worked in Bettiah among the women and children. George also observes that in the earlier stage of AoG mission female missionaries outnumbered men.[65] The Mission Center concentrated on girls' education. At one time there were 100 girls in the orphanage.

In 1936 the first AoG church was built in Bettiah and the Men's Bible School in Chapra was started in 1950 by Rev. Paul Shoemaker. After some years the first Indian Principal of the Bible School was

---

[62] Samuel, *Christhuvil Oru Samarppitha Jeevitham,* 165-167.

[63] Samuel, *Christhuvil Oru Samarppitha Jeevitham,* 174.

[64] S.D. Ponraj, *From Graveyard to Vineyard: Transformation in Bihar (The Historical Development, 1790-2008)*, 59.

[65] George, *Trailblazers for God,* 125.

Rev. Paul Sharma. Later both the women and men's Bible schools were shifted to Hardoi in Uttar Pradesh. This could be one of the reasons for the lack of indigenous leadership for the AoG Church in Bihar. Later Finish Pentecostal Church in Toronto, Canada, sent Esther Greus and Eva Rinny sent to Bihar for mission works and they planted the first church in Purnea in 1952. The same mission later became Salem Pentecostal Church of North India. Their main work was among the Santal tribal people in Purnia, Araria and Katihar Districts of North East Bihar.[66]

As we turn to the state of Uttar Pradesh, as we have already seen, in the period before and after 1920's the Western as well as the Indian Pentecostal missionaries were active in proclaiming the Pentecostal message which resulted in the formation of some churches and mission activities in the state. In 1942, at Nishadganj, Mahanagr in Luknow Pastor B.M. Chand, established a church called *Dua Ka Ghar*. This church became a centre of Pentecostal mission and sent missionaries to other states of North India and established Pentecostal churches. It was the leading church in the state of Uttar Pradesh in the 1950's. Similarly, in the city of Agra, two evangelists, Christy Liddle and Harry Liddle were working independently. In 1930, Pasto M.K. Chacko visited there and established Pentecostal mission and many people joined him. He then handed over the mission to the two evangelists and moved to Delhi. The work began to flourish under them and they felt the need of a training institution to equip the native people to preach gospel and plant churches. They began a Bible school in Agra and later in 1960 shifted to Dehra Doon which is known as the Doon Bible College.

The Pentecostal message was brought to Rajasthan for the first time by Pentecostal missionaries from other states of North India.[67] According to Wessley Lukose, a Mr. and Mrs. Jiwa brought the Pentecostal message to Rajasthan for the first time in the 1930s to the district of Banaswara. Mr. Jiwa was a native of Jawara, Piplod, in Madhya Pradesh state, who married a girl from the Mukti Mission run by Pandita Ramabai. She had an experience of the Holy Spirit

[66] Ponraj, *From Graveyard to Vineyard,* 61.

[67] Wessly Lukose, "Pentecostal Beginnings in Rajasthan: Part One," *AJPS* 12:2 (2009): 243.

baptism with speaking in tongues, a recipient from the Mukti revival. They did not establish any Pentecostal churches, but were involved in vigorous evangelistic activities. Another person who brought Pentecostal message to Rajasthan in the next decade was Peter Lal, a native Pentecostal missionary from UP, came to work in the district of Ajmer in 1942. He was sent as a missionary from the *Dua ka Ghar* (the House of Prayer), Lucknow, UP. As already mentioned, *Dhua ka Khar* is an indigenous Pentecostal church established by a local Pentecostal minister, B.M. Chand. Lal extensively travelled and preached the Pentecostal message in various parts of the state, such as Jodhpur, Jaipur, Kota and Udaipur.[68]

After 1960, slowly more and more missionaries from Kerala began to enter into various parts of the north and established Pentecostal churches. Later Pentecostal missionaries from Tamil Nadu also joined in Pentecostal mission activities which we shall explore in the next chapter. This gives us an outline of Pentecostal work in the period running from 1920 and 1960. There were not many churches, however, some people preserved Pentecostal activities intact in different locations which enabled later missionaries to make those places their bases. Now we shall turn into the most important era of North Indian Pentecostal history, one which saw major growth.

[68] Lukose, "Pentecostal Beginnings in Rajasthan," 244-247.

Chapter 6

North Indian Pentecostal History (1960-2010)

A new era in the history of Pentecostalism in north India began after 1960; Pentecostalism began to spread its roots deep down into the hard soil of the north. The outpouring of the Spirit and the resultant revivals and mission in different parts of North India had watered the spiritual wilderness and new sprouts of greenery, in the form of Pentecostal congregations, began to raise their heads here and there. The next 50 years of the North Indian Pentecostal history were generous in growth and multiplication of the movement. It is impossible to look into each and every state of the north in this work; instead we will outline important milestones and growth, selectively. As noted earlier, most western missionaries had left India by 1947 and the control of all churches came into the hands of Indian leadership. However, in the case of the Pentecostal movement, there were only a few churches, especially in the states like Uttar Pradesh, Punjab, Rajasthan, Gujarat, Madhya Pradesh and Maharashtra so on. For example, quoting Shinde, George states that until 1970 the growth of AoG churches which had established Pentecostal network in the north was marginal. The total number of believers was less than 4,000 and before 1974, the number of churches was only 90. The believers from non-Christian background were 1,038 and the biological growth brought only 582 people into the church.[1]

[1] George, *Trailblazers for God,* 193.

Nevertheless, the south had experienced major Pentecostal growth and many young people began to move towards the north with the Pentecostal message as explained in the previous chapter. Besides, a new brand of North Indian Pentecostal missionaries who carried out significant mission work in the hard terrains of the north, especially among Tribals and Dalits also began to emerge in the horizon.

We should note down that, it was not solely by the effort of the south Indian missionaries that great Pentecostal move was occurred, but some of the overwhelming outpouring of revival fire upon native north Indian people, especially upon Dalits and Tribals groups were because of the sacrificial works of native missionaries. These outpourings of the Spirit upon native people as the testimonies show, were God-sent and God used some ordinary people for such great events. Later, the south Indian Pentecostal pioneers could consolidate those revivals into church growth. Thus, it is a story of divine as well as human endeavours culminating and the south and the north united that wrote a magnificent story of Pentecostal history in north India. This does not mean that everything was rosy and smooth; there were quarrels and splits and at the same time unity and fellowship. Here also we need to apply the principle, what Bergunder calls, 'the historical connections and synchronous interrelations' and also 'the diachronous network.'[2]

It is also important to mention that since 1960s more and more Pentecostal missionaries from major Pentecostal denominations of the south began to establish their churches in north India. This was not happening by planned church planting programmes or by targeted mission strategies to reach unreached places but as we have seen, individual missionaries taking steps to evangelise north Indian soil because of the 'burden' for north India. The examples we have seen in the last chapter like Kurian Thomas and P.S. Samuel and many others coming their own and planting churches. However, they have established their own mission organisations and churches, not having any formal relation with the denominations they belonged to back in Kerala. Through their work, a strand of Pentecostal churches and mission were established with south Indian Pentecostal doctrines at the core but with some difference in their approach toward church

[2] Bergunder, "Constructing Indian Pentecostalism," 189-191.

planting and external practices. For instance, in Kerala, Pentecostal denominations strictly prohibited use of ornaments and believers are encouraged to wear white dresses in worship and other occasions. However, in the north, these leaders did not follow such strict code of conduct owing to the cultural underpinnings. Moreover, they had trained native people for mission and through them church planting momentum had accelerated.

Later, more Kerala Pentecostal missionaries from major denominations like Indian Pentecostal Church (IPC), Church of God reached north India by their own initiative and established churches and later affiliated with their respective mother churches in Kerala. Later, however, these denominations of the south especially from Kerala began to send their own missionaries to the north. They have established Pentecostal churches with the same doctrines and practices. It is to be noted that AoG churches were existing in the north but those were few in numbers. But the coming of the Kerala Pentecostal missionaries of AoG had resulted in the fast growth of the denomination. In later stage, missionaries from The Sharon Fellowship Church, The New India Church of God and other denominations began to send their trained church planters to north India. Now each of these denominations have organised in state and regional levels and they carry out their own mission activities. Thus, we find hundreds of churches of these of denominations in almost all the north Indian states and in major cities.

It is also to be noted that some of these churches still target people from Kerala state who have been settled in north India. For example, we can see hundreds of such Malayalam language churches of IPC, Church of God, The Sharon Fellowship and so on, in Mumbai, Delhi and many other major north Indian urban centres. Later, missionaries from Tamil Nadu who belonged these Pentecostal denominations and independent Tamil Pentecostal movements planted Tamil churches targeting Tamil people in the north Indian cities. Here we will not be able discuss the extent and growth of branches of these major Pentecostal denominational churches owing to the limitation of space and time. We will treat them as a whole in north Indian context. However, we need to note that they also played significant role in the growth of north Indian Pentecostal movement.

Their presence, outreach and financial support for mission have helped in the formation of many north Indian language churches. They have sent out south Indian and north Indian missionaries to villages and towns to evangelise and this has resulted in major Pentecostal growth and formation of new mission agencies.

Taking these above mentioned factors, we will try to bring out a picture of what had happened in this era, especially how local revivals and the subsequent mission endeavours contributed to the growth of the movement in the following pages. At least up to the 1970s we are compelled to depend on the biographies of some of the South Indian Pentecostals. For later stage, after the 70s, we have certain information, albeit in oral tradition. However, for the latest stage, it is almost impossible to comprehend and describe all the mission activities, as many of them are unknown and multiplying day by day. In addition, it is also risky because of the unsettled conditions Pentecostals still face in North India.

Rajasthan

Although foreign missionaries worked among the Tribals of Rajasthan, there were no Pentecostal churches. However, certain revivals occurred in Udaipur and Banswara, although people did not know them to be Spirit-awakenings.[3] In the Shepherd Memorial Church (CNI) of Udaipur in 1959-60, a powerful revival arose through Emmanuel Loel, an Air Force officer from Jabalpur, M.P. They were speaking in tongues and falling on the ground in the presence of God and it was K.V. Philip, a missionary from Kerala who in 1960 explained these as the works of the Spirit. Philip was one of the early Pentecostal missionaries to Rajasthan.

Another powerful outpouring of the Spirit was occurred in 1965-67 in Banswara. A few young people – Praveen, Tajendra Masih and Sohan Lal – were praying in a medical store and, suddenly the power of the Spirit came upon them and all of them fell down from their chairs and began to speak in tongues. Later they began to gather every night in the CNI Mission hostel for young boys and

[3] For a full description see Lukose, "A Contextual Missiology,"' 103-126.

many more people received Spirit-baptism. However, these revivals did not materialise in church-planting.[4]

Pastor M.K. Chacko, whose story explored in the last chapter, engaged in evangelistic activities in Rajasthan. In December 1963, he concentrated on his work in Jaipur, the capital of the state, for six months and thus established the first Pentecostal church in the city. Later, one of Chacko's north Indian disciples, Claude Roberts from Delhi, took charge of this church, which was called the "Full Gospel Church."[5]

It was the coming of Thomas Mathews to Udaipur in 1963, after the mission call of K.V. Philip that made an important milestone in the history of North Indian Pentecostalism.[6] Mathews visited these places and explained the biblical and theological legitimacy of the Pentecostal experience. Some of the young people who experienced Spirit-baptism joined him and began to work among the Tribal groups in Banswara, Udaipur and other places. The untiring works of Mathews and his co-workers, like Tajendra Masih, Pathas Masih, Valu Singh and many others, resulted in church growth in predominantly tribal areas. In the beginning of his ministry, he had been with Kurian Thomas of Itarsi; however, later he parted from him and developed his own church planting activities.

One of the valuable contributions of Mathews can be explained in terms of harnessing the church growth movement which was initiated by local revivals, which were about to extinguish.[7] He had trained local missionaries and pastors to reach inaccessible regions of Rajasthan, Gujarat, Madhya Pradesh and other various north Indian states. This band of sacrificial and dedicated local missionaries who were real heroes carried Pentecostal message in the interior regions of north India that resulted in magnificent growth of the movement. Under his leadership, the Native Missionary Movement began to

[4] Lukose, "A Contextual Missiology," 111-113.

[5] Chacko, *An Autobiography,* 32.

[6] Thonnakkal, *Marubhoomiyile Appostalan*, 46; Kaithamangalam, *Marubhoomiyil Thalarathu,* 17; Simmons, *Vision Mission,* 26. His life and missionary activities are vividly portrayed in these books.

[7] Finny Philip, "The Thomas Mathews Revolution," *Cross and Crown* 36/1 (November 05-March 2006): 18-23.

accelerate the church growth and gather momentum; the churches are now called Filadelfia Fellowship Churches. He also began a Bible college for training native missionaries in Udaipur, Rajasthan; now the movement boasts more than 1,300 congregations spread across 14 states in India. The mission also runs a number of schools, orphanages and Bible schools in different states of North India. It is also involved in medical help, self-help groups in villages for the poor and destitute, film and literature ministries.[8]

Later, Pentecostal missionaries from the south Indian state of Tamil Nadu also began to work in different districts of Rajasthan, especially among the tribal people. Along with these missionaries, local people also began to plant churches and run mission organisations. Many local missionaries from tribal background set up church planting ministries.

Gujarat and Maharashtra

There were some revivals in Gujarat and Maharashtra. One among them was through George Thomas Paradeshi, who had a special gift as regards healing and exorcism; he came to Nadiad in Gujarat in 1970's. Such was the conviction and the spiritual revival, that on one day while Thomas Paradeshi and his friends were giving thanks over breakfast, the Holy Spirit came mightily upon them and hearing the noise, people began pouring in from everywhere. Everyone, who came near the veranda, began to fall down and confess their sins and filled with the Holy Spirit.[9] Later on the revival spread to Ahmadabad. Some CNI Pastors took immersion baptism under the hands of Paradeshi secretly. There are instances when few took baptism during night in overhead water tank of their houses to make it a secret affair. According to Joseph, the spiritual revival kindled in the ministry of Paradeshi faded in the long run because he did not establish churches with the new converts. However in the 20th century it was Thomas Paradeshi, whom God used mightily as a man of God having healing power and power over demons, and

---

[8] Roger Simmons, *Vision, Mission and a Movement* (Udaipur, Rajasthan: Native Missionary Movement, 2008), 131.

[9] Joseph, "Dolka Revival and After;" Philip, "The Thomas Mathew's Revolution," 20; Mathew, *Kerala Penthecosthu Charithram,* 191.

charismatic preacher not only in Gujarat, but also in different parts of North India right from Bengal to Gujarat in those days. It was said that through him many had accepted the Pentecostal message. His first convert was Joshua G. Raj, a Medical Practitioner in the Nadiad Methodist Mission Hospital. When Dr. Raj received immersion baptism, he had to pay a high price; he was sacked from his job. He came to Ahmadabad with his family and acquired a house in Maninagar Christian Hill Society. He got himself registered as a medical doctor, began a Dawakhana (Dispensary) in the Gomtipur area, which later on became a Duvakhana (House of Prayer).[10] Later Raj became a powerful missionary in Ahmadabad and also in surrounding tribal areas. Paradeshi and Raj used to visit eastern Surat, Dang and Navapur in Maharashtra frequently for missionary work in the seventies and eighties. However, the spiritual revival kindled in the ministry of Paradeshi and Raj faded in the long run because it did not establish churches.[11]

Another revival took place in Pipal Kuah and Navapur, small tribal villages in the border of Gujarat and Maharashtra in 1970, which resulted in the widespread growth of Pentecostalism in those areas of the tribal belt. There were foreign mission agencies, like the Alliance Mission and the Brethren Mission working among the Tribals.[12] However, there were no Pentecostal churches. On 20 November 1970, P.D. Benjamin along with Raj, came to Pipal Kuah.[13] According to Shanmukh Patel, Benjamin was so powerful that evil spirits would go away from people even in nearby places. He had special gift to pray for couple having no children.[14] In Navapur,

---

[10] Joseph, "Dolka Revival and After."

[11] Joseph, "Dolka Revival and After."

[12] In 1932, Brethren missionaries began working in those parts of Gujarat and Maharashtra and some natives like Boridas Narayan Patel also became prominent leaders. Later, his son Shanmukh Bhai Patel became a powerful instrument in revival and church-growth in tribal areas. Shanmukh Patel, interview, Pipal Kuah, 10 August 2009 and Philip, "The Thomas Mathew's Revolution," 20.

[13] According to Shanmukh Bhai Patel, Benjamin was from the Garwal area in Uttar Pradesh and we know that he was working in Indian Railways in Punjab. He had a Christian Ashram in Meerut. Also see Thomas, *God's Trailblazer,* 26.

[14] S. Patel, interview, Pipal Kuah, 10 August 2009.

people like Pandhu Bhai, Ranji Bhai and others became leaders. Shanmukh Patel, from Pipal Kuah was also filled with the Spirit. Then he began to take the revival fire to nearby places. His sister and other women were also with him in ministry. His sister's name is Lingi Bhai and her husband and others used to conduct meetings.[15] He was working with the Brethren and the CNI[16] churches.

In Vyara, one of the meetings by Shanmukh Patel became a place of great outpouring of the Spirit. According to him, he was conducting a meeting in the CNI church after his Spirit-baptism. There were some people gathered and the manifestation of the Spirit occurred with voice and the walls of the church began to tremble. Hearing this commotion, people from the town gathered in the church and the Spirit convicted all of them and most of them who were non-Christian Tribals or Hindus. Then those gathered were convicted of their sins and began to cry in loud voices. Those who repented began to speak in other tongues, saw vision and prophesied. There was a great move of the spirit and the revival events continued for several weeks. He claims that, within seven days, he had baptised almost 3,500 people there and that, in his lifetime, he baptised more than 38,000 people.[17]

Even dead people were raised and many were healed through his ministry. Shanmukh Bhai Patel narrated a particular incident. One evening outside his church in Pipal Kuah, he was conducting a meeting. A group of people were carrying a dead woman in a bullock-cart to their village. One who was driving the cart said that they would attend the meeting. They kept the dead body inside the church and joined the meeting. There was a powerful manifestation of the Holy Spirit. After a while to their surprise, the dead woman came out of the church and joined in the meeting clapping her hands and jumping. The woman and her relatives gave testimonies in the meeting and such incidents led to conversion of many people.

---

[15] These were predominantly tribal areas – Ahwa, Vapi, Vyara, Umed, Utwada, Dharmpur, Nanapeda, Motapada – and churches were established in all these places; S. Patel, interview, Pipal Kuah, 10 August 2009.

[16] CNI stands for Churches of North India, a group of denominational churches.

[17] S. Patel, interview, Pipal Kuah, 10 August 2009.

According to Patel, this revival helped to proclaim Jesus as the only Saviour in those areas.[18] Later Dr. Raj and another missionary, Elison Joseph, worked in those areas and brought many people to spiritual awakening. However, neither Kurien Thomas nor the biographers of Thomas Mathews mentioned these revivals or the pioneers.

The Pentecostal mission continued in these areas by native missionaries without any assistance but some churches were established. In 1981, Thomas Mathews along with his friends visited these areas. When they reached Gujarat, according to Mathews, through a vision, they were directed to a particular house in a village called Raniamba in Ukai. Before their arrival, Gargi, the man of the household, had a vision that five people would be arriving from Rajasthan.[19] Staying there, they conducted several meetings and many miracles were reported; as a result, churches were established. Once a dead child was raised through prayer in a village and this event helped to open door for the Pentecostal message in those regions.[20] Under the leadership of Mathews' wife Mary Mathews, many women evangelists toured many of the villages in this region that impacted the lives of the women of interior villages spiritually as well as socially.[21] Later Mathews moved to Navapur and people who had already been revived in the earlier revivals joined Mathews. Today Navapur is a centre of Pentecostal mission and has the greatest Christian convention in North India under the Filadelfia Church. It has been claimed that almost 50,000 people gather there each year for a few days.[22]

Similarly, Dr. Raj's movement also began to grow but was divided into two: one is headed by Raj's grandson, the International Full Gospel Church which has more than 100 churches while the other branch, known as Calvary Sangh, claims about 75 churches. Pastor Navneet Gamit has a church with more than 3,000 members in Vyara. The Fellowship Ashram Church of Saji Mathew claims

---

[18] S. Patel, interview, Pipal Kuah, 10 August 2009.

[19] Simmons, *Vision Mission*, 71-72.

[20] Simmons, *Vision Mission*, 73.

[21] Simmons, *Vision Mission*, 75-78.

[22] Glory M. Philip, "Celestial Celebration of Saints: Navapur "07," *Cross and Crown* 37/2 (November-December 2007): 11-16.

to have mission works in almost 150 villages in Gujarat. The Joy Ministry of Vijay Gamit has about 100 churches. George Philip claims more than 100 churches. Moreover, there are many other missions working among the Tribals and all those places are 'Pentecostal' now.[23] Similarly, in Maharashtra, the Maharashtra Village Ministry, the Mahanaidhan Ministry, the Indian Christian Movement and many others have strong native bases. The AoG Marathi also has extensive church activities in Maharashtra while Pastor Peter Desilva in Pune has more than 10,000 members in a single church. Another Pentecostal mission in Nagpur began in 1993 by Saji Lukose which is known as the Mission India has several churches in north India, runs several Bible schools for training evangelists and other charity works.

Another important milestone in the history of the Pentecostal movement in the north especially in Mumbai, Maharashtra began with the beginning of the New Life Fellowship. The New Life Fellowship was born in 1968 in Bombay by Pastor S. Joseph from Mariapura a small village situated on the out skirts of Bangalore, in the South of India. Joseph came to the city of Bombay in 1950 and endured a hard life living on the streets of Bombay. As his testimony goes, dissatisfied with life and seeking answers to life's questions, God met with him. This encounter radically changed his life. He became the ordained pastor of the New Life Centre Church in Mumbai in 1969, a self supporting church started by missionaries from New Zealand. The church had been aiming to be a mega-church in the city but till 1980 only grown into less than hundred people. Joseph and some of his colleagues spent time in prayer and fasting and the Lord gave them a different vision. Then the mega-church plan was metamorphosed into a plan for 'hundreds of churches' in the city. By 1989 there were more than 1500 house churches in Bombay with overall congregations of over 12,000.[24]

Four levels of meetings are mentioned in NLF's vision documents. Celebration Centres and Sunday services, house

---

[23] As Bergunder commented, many of them were split and formed new organisations; see Bergunder, *The South Indian Pentecostal,* 12-13.

[24] Hedlund, "Indigenous Pentecostalism in India," 231.

churches, outreach centres and prayer groups. A house church consists of at least ten committed members having communion and taking offering. All the groups participate in praise and worship, teaching of scripture, manifestation of the gifts of the Spirit. The movement does not hold properties in the city. The house groups meets in homes or rented quarters. Even the church offices work in rented houses. In an antagonistic and pluralistic context, this concept is advantageous as there is little to be destroyed in case of a violent persecution.[25] Moreover, in sky-rocketing property market in Mumbai, resources can be directed to mission and church planting instead of property. There are other leaders who worked along with Joseph. Pastor Willie, who has been a part of the NLF since 1973, Shelton Davidson started in 1977, Jerry D'Souza in 1980 and Shekar Kallianpur in 1981. Each of these pastors was responsible for a region of Mumbai.[26]

In 1990s NLF experienced tremendous growth in Bombay and throughout India. In May 1992, a special outreach effort in Bombay resulted in 6000 people joining the movement.[27] In 1995 the Chembur (Mumbai) NLF church began an outreach in Sholapur district and many miraculous healings were reported. Within a year more than 2,500 people joined the movement and 24 Sholapur villages have seen springing up of new churches where there were no churches. During five months in 1997 the movement sent 719 missionaries into 12 important cities which resulted in more than 35,000 people joining the movement.[28] The same year, the Reach India Project targeted 12 cities with more than 1,500 workers. An estimated 2.6 million homes were visited and 1,600 believed. In 1998 the aim was to adopt 1,000 villages and to establish house churches in each village.[29]

NLF was also involved in various areas social activities such as housing, employment, healthcare, schooling, *balavadis* (child care) and different other projects. The New Life Medical and Educational

---

[25] Mikel Neumann, *Home Groups for Urban Cultures* (Pasadena, California: William Carey Library, 1999), 7.

[26] Neumann, *Home Groups for Urban Cultures,* 8.

[27] Mikel Neumann, *Home Groups for Urban Cultures,* 6-7.

[28] Hedlund, "Indigenous Pentecostalism in India," 232.

[29] Hedlund, "Indigenous Pentecostalism in India," 231.

Trust provide medical care and operate free schools for the poor. In Dharavi, Asia's largest slum, NLF provides medicines, food and soap. Slums are the hubs of alcoholism, drug addiction, abuse of women and children and starvation. Here house churches have been formed and free education is provided to many of the poor and exploited children.[30]

The New Life Fellowship had been a trailblazer in the realm of Pentecostal and charismatic church growth in north India for a period of 30 years till 2010. However, in 2010 a split took place in NLF and according to Joseph, 2010 was a challenging year of change and realignment, resulted in 'turning point' in his life and ministry. Subsequent to a leadership challenge, in May 2010, New Life Movement International (NLMI) was birthed. Leaders, churches and ministries that choose to remain under his leadership were realigned under NLMI. The Churches are now known as New Life Church.

Punjab

Similarly Punjab also experienced revivals in the districts of Gurdaspur, Ferozpur and other places which are predominantly Dalit areas in the 1970s. It was through Imdad Masih that the movement began in Gurdaspur and many were healed, delivered of evil spirits, while the dead were raised. Around 1978, he came to Ferozpur and conducted meetings in a CNI church where there was a great revival. There he appointed Babu Kalidas, David Hawel and C.M. Rustum in charge of the churches he established. Throughout Punjab, many people were saved through his ministry and became Pentecostal leaders; later, these people consolidated the movement.[31]

Another person who became instrumental for the Pentecostal revival in the Punjab in the 1980's was Karamchand, from Ferozpur. His mother was transformed by Imdad Masih's Ministry. He was a policeman and drunkard and used to trouble his mother. However, she was earnest in her prayer for him and, one night he had a vision of Jesus while he was on duty. Then he fasted for 21 days and began

---

[30] Hedlund, "Indigenous Pentecostalism in India," 232.

[31] Pastor Pyarelal, interview by author, Udaipur, Rajasthan, 25 August 2009.

to evangelise all those areas. Many miracles occurred as a result of his ministry while churches were also established. Then he joined the Church of God through Pastor John Samuel. However, after 3 years he began his own church called *Atmik Masih Sangati.* He was one of the pioneers in the Pentecostal mission in Punjab.[32] He even moved into states like Himachal Pradesh, Madhya Pradesh and as far as the south, Andhra Pradesh.

Now, there are many major indigenous and established Pentecostal churches like the Church of God, the Assemblies of God, and the Indian Pentecostal Church in the districts of Ludhiana, Jullundher, Patiala, Gurdaspur, and Dhariwal. For instance, in Ferozpur, Pastor Bod Masih has more than 2,500 members in a single church and almost 40 pastors working under him in different areas. Similarly, in Gurdaspur, Munir Masih boasts of having almost 3,500 members in a single church. In Dhariwal he has extensive works as well. Obviously, the Pentecostal movement is growing in Punjab.

Madhya Pradesh

There were some Pentecostal churches in different cities of Madhya Pradesh, for example, in the early 1960s, Pastor O.J. Wilson began a Pentecostal church in Jabalpur; however, it was after 1984 that a widespread Pentecostal revival occurred in tribal areas. In Indore, Dhinakaran, a famous healing evangelist from the south conducted a meeting in 1984, and many people received Spirit-baptism.[33] A woman called Anitabehn and some others were instrumental in bringing a church growth movement among the Tribal people. People like Sunderlal, Vikolson, Kanyalal and Amos Singh worked among the Tribals of M.P. and established churches. Another person, Rajesh Jain worked among Jain people in Jabhua city and converted many

---

[32] Pyarelal worked with Karamchand for 13 years.

[33] D.G.S. Dhinakaran of Jesus Call's Ministry, see more about Dhinakaran; Michael Bergunder, "Ministry of Compassion:" D.G.S. Dhinakaran, 'Christian Healer-Prophet from Tamilnadu," *Christianity is Indian,* 161-177; Also see for his theology, Ghanakan C.G., "Charismata and Compassion: Dhinakaran, Charismatic Healing and Pastoral Pentecostalism in South-India – A Practical Assessment," (Unpublished PhD Thesis, University of Birmingham, Birmingham, 2006).

people. Slowly the movement began to grow into the tribal districts of Jabhua, Barwani, Khargone, Dhar, and Khandwa.[34]

In the 90s, there was rapid Pentecostal growth in these places. The Native Missionary Movement by Thomas Mathews has planted number of churches in tribal regions of Madhya Pradesh. Blessing Youth Mission by R. Stanley and team is involved in revival retreats, Bible study seminars, discipleship and leadership training programmes, outreaches in villages and tribal areas, medical and relief works, homes and schools for tribal children and church planting in MP and other states of North India. The Indian Evangelical Team by P.G. Vargis has church planting as well as missionary training centre in Madhya Pradesh. Another Pentecostal movement, the Jesus Mission by Saju Mathew and James has targeted local people in Damoh and other states since 1994.[35] Now, Jesus Mission is having missionaries in many of the north Indian states and claims to have more than 150 missionary families involved in evangelism, church planting, children homes, school, vernacular printing, Bible training, charity and literacy programs. The Susamachar Seva Mandali, Bhopal, by Samuel Matthai has several branch churches in Madhya Pradesh and in other states. It also runs a Theological Seminary in Bhopal called Susamachar Theological College and Seminary. Now there are many missions working in these places and hundreds of churches have been established.

Bihar

Pastor K. T. Eapen, a graduate of Hindustan Bible Institute (HBI), Chennai, was one of those early pioneers in Bihar. He came to Bihar as early as 1964 along with his newly married wife, Chinnamma. His first mission field was Purnia working with the two lady missionaries who were sent by Finish Pentecostal Church. After working in several parts of North Bihar, Pastor Eapen finally came to Patna in January 1965 with a burden to preach the gospel and reach the unreached people. He was regularly involved in the distribution of gospel literature and street preaching. The Lord used him to bring several

[34] Ankur Masih, interview, Udaipur, Rajasthan, 3 September 2009.

[35] http://jesusmissionindia.org/aboutus.aspx. (accessed 10/07/2014).

influential people to Himself in Patna. He established the House of Prayer.[36]

Just as we have explored in chapter two, the Operation and Mobilization Teams came to Bihar in the year 1965. OM Teams had their office in Ranchi and worked all over the then united Bihar. As Ponraj puts it, "their pioneering mission work in Bihar during the three decades (1960-90) was ploughing the land (preparing the hearts of the people) and the sowing the seeds of the gospel (through literature and open air preaching). Today the great harvest that we have in Bihar is the direct result of their faithful work." Similarly, India Every Home Crusade came to Bihar in 1976. IEHC was primarily involved in the distribution of Gospel tracts in every home systematically. Later the seekers were followed up with camps and correspondence courses.[37] Hundreds of people who heard the gospel through such mission agencies responded to Pentecostal missionaries and several churches are being planted in Bihar.

Another important Pentecostal move in the state of Bihar and surrounding states happened through the Gospel Echoing Missionary Society (GEMS). Several indigenous mission agencies work in Bihar-Jarkhand and one of the notables, and of Pentecostal type, is the GEMS which began in 1972 by the GEMS House of Prayer at Chrompet, Chennai of Augustine Jebakumar. Its concentrated mission effort has resulted in the formation of several churches and mission activities where there were no churches.[38]

Even though Jebakumar and family belonged to a denominational church they experienced the Pentecostal power and started practising in their day to day ministry. Many young people joined from South India with a passion to reach the unreached areas of Bihar and north India. This resulted in establishing churches and missions and created a momentum in many part of Bihar especially in Bhojpuri, Magahi & Maithili speaking areas. Later it grew as a major reckoning force in the harvest field due to their innovative models in reaching several thousand children and young people. In turn they even started Schools and Day Care Centres in big number.

---

[36] Ponraj, *From Graveyard to Vineyard,* 64.

[37] Ponraj, *From Graveyard to Vineyard,* 64.

[38] Hedlund, "Indigenous Pentecostalism in India," 230.

GEMS today has more than 80% of its missionaries from North India and moves with the vision for their fourth decade as "towards exponential growth."[39]

According to the information available the GEMS mission is growing rapidly with more than 2000 workers in 690 stations with 1035 worshipping centers in Bihar, Jharkand, Uttar Pradesh, Madhya Pradesh and Maharashtra.[40] Many projects are carried out including 48 children's homes plus a home for 100 children of stonecutters and a home for 60 children suffering from polio. GEMS also operates 118 Hindi Medium schools and 11 English schools including a high school. It runs various development projects in villages, nursing school, industrial training centre and so on. Out of 69 linguistic dialects in Bihar, GEMS concentrates mainly on three major Hindi dialects of Bhojpuri, Maitali and Magai. Based in Rohdas District, the Mission works mainly in neglected areas of North Bihar, Central and West Bihar. It is also involves in medical mission, education and social services including rescuing of children from bonded labour.[41]

Another important Pentecostal mission move took place in the state of Bihar through the establishment of India Mission by Dr Mathew P. Koshy and Dr. K.T. Joseph in 1993. Through a vision they were led to Bihar to begin a mission work. In 1994, a worship centre was started at Hajipur along with a Bible training centre to train evangelists. Later in 2000, Dr. Aby P. Mathew joined India Mission and his efforts resulted in the rapid growth of mission endeavours and the movement spread to different districts of Bihar adding more and more people. The focus of India Mission is to reach unreached areas and plant churches which are self-governing and self-supporting. It is also involved in the ministries of running children homes, mercy ministries, film shows and so on. At present the mission claims more than thousand missionaries working in different parts of Bihar.

Several Pentecostal churches and mission agencies are active today in Bihar, Jarkhand and surrounding states; they include the Church of God, Ceylon Pentecostal Mission, Full Gospel Church, Full Gospel New Testament Church, Indian Pentecostal Church,

---

[39] Ponraj, *From Graveyard to Vineyard,* 65-66.

[40] http://www.gemsbihar.org/index.php/aboutus/history (accessed 10/07/2014).

[41] Hedlund, "Indigenous Pentecostalism in India," 230.

Maranatha Church, Pentecostal Assembly Church, Pentecostal Bethel Church Association, Pentecostal Church of God, Salem Christian Church, Salem Pentecostal Church, and others.[42]

The Himalayan Regions

Another successful move in the north Indian Pentecostal mission was inaugurated by the coming of P.M. Thomas to Udhampur in the state of Jammu-Kashmir in 1963. The state is a mountainous region and the challenge of this vast and rugged region of the Himalayas with extreme climatic conditions and recent terrorist activities make the state an impervious target for missionaries. There had been missionary presence in these regions; up to 200 missionaries worked there at one time. The CMS, Scottish Presbyterian Church, the Central Asia Mission and Moravians had been there in different locations of the Himalayas but had to leave after India's independence in 1947.

Leaving his comfortable life in Kerala, Thomas began his mission on November 17, 1963, at Udhampur in a tiny mud hut in a government land; that was his house, church, kitchen and everything in the early years. Thomas along with several associates focused on the unreached areas of the Himalayan region including Nepal, Sikkim and Bhutan. His untiring work has resulted in planting of several churches, schools and missionary training institutions. He faced various levels of oppositions and the constructions of the churches were opposed by some hard-line religious elements in the state.

Even though he came from Anglican tradition, he experienced the baptism of the Holy Spirit and took believer's baptism under Shankaru Abraham, whom Thomas calls 'the apostle of the Jammu Mountains'. This event had kindled a great revival among the members of the congregation in October 1971 and some people were being baptised.[43] The revival continued on to 1973 and through special gospel meetings more and more people began to join the church. The same year the Kashmir Evangelical Fellowship was formed and nine missionaries joined Thomas' team and a couple

---

[42] Hedlund, "Indigenous Pentecostalism in India," 230.

[43] John Lindner, *The Mountain Shall Sing: The Story of P.M. Thomas and Himalaya Evangelical Mission* (Gorakhpur, India: Himalaya Evangelical Mission, 2003), 56-58.

of new churches had been established. Several missionaries began trekking different areas of Himalayan regions and north India and proclaimed the gospel message. The women team led by two sisters from Kerala Kunjumol and Kunjoonjamma visited many schools and touched the lives of boys, girls and teachers with the gospel of Jesus Christ.[44] The move of the Spirit begun in 1971 continued into 1975 and beyond, carried by a wave of signs and miracles. Thomas and his friends also concentrated their mission efforts among Kashmiri refugees who were displaced by India Pakistan war. Many people accepted the gospel message.[45]

In 1978 Several new missionaries were added and a dozen of Bible Seminary students and others joined the ministry.[46] The Soram Evangelical Fellowship from Mizoram sent two sisters, Moithe and Ringi. A church building was constructed in Ramnagar in 1979.[47] Several Pentecostal crusades were conducted in strategically important centres where the new missionaries were sent. In Banihal, a Muslim dominated area among the mountains where Ninan Zachariah was working, an evil spirit possessed man was completely delivered. Four men were holding his hand and they brought him in front of the stage. When he was prayed in the name of Jesus, and rebuked the evil spirits, he screamed aloud and soon the evil spirits left him. This miraculous event had a positive effect upon the people. Next morning all five of them came for the Bible class. After the class the Moulavi invited Thomas to his Mazjid and had a blessed time of sharing the gospel with him.[48] Another crusade was conducted at Billawar a Hindu dominated area where Bro. Soman was sent. A girl who could not open her mouth for 15 days opened her mouth wide when prayed. Today there is a strong church in Billawar. The

---

[44] Lindner, *The Mountain Shall Sing*, 74-78.

[45] Lindner, *The Mountain Shall Sing*, 85-86.

[46] Thus, Soman was placed at Billawar, Ninan Zachariah at Banihal, Joseph and James at Ramban, Stephen at Qazigund, Varghese at Ramgad, Georgekutty at Jammu at Nagrotta, Danish at Nagrotta Gujroo, Joy at Jindra, Joseph at Hiranagar, Sam and Esa at Meeran Sahib.

[47] P. M. Thomas, "Old Memories (1975-1980)," *Himalaya Harvest* (XXXII/4 December 2011).

[48] Thomas, "Old Memories (1975-1980)."

number of the believers among the Doda mountains alone has now crossed 700.[49]

In 1984 the outreach ministry began to spread all over the places like Kishenpur, Billawar, Ramnagar, Cheneni, Katra, Riasi, and nearby mountains. The evangelistic team also began to distribute relief items like blankets and food materials to Kashmiri refugees.[50] In 1986 Kashmir Mission Institute was began to train missionaries.[51] In 1987 the first mission station was established in Ladakh which lies five to twelve thousand feet altitude and temperature goes down to -20 to -30. Another mission station was opened in Kargil with a special focus on Tibetan Buddhists.[52] By the year 1989, more and more missionaries joined the movement and even in the midst of terrorist activities in Punjab the mission began to grow. More and more mission stations were opened in different parts of Kashmir and Punjab. In later years mission was spread into Madhya Pradesh, Maharashtra, Orissa, Bihar, Uttar Pradesh, Sikkim, West Bengal Uttarakhand and other north Indian states.[53]

In 1987, while Thomas was hospitalised in Kerala, some of the co-workers 'conspired' against him. According to him, these leaders alleged that he was hiding the mission fund in his private account. This resulted in a court case but Thomas was found innocent the court cases were withdrawn. However, this episode resulted in 29 missionaries resigning from the movement and the formation of another movement called 'Gospel for Kashmir'. At the end Thomas was left with only three missionaries. Within few months the newly formed organisation was broken and all were scattered.[54] According to Thomas, misguided brethren from within tried to wrest the ministry from his control. At least a dozen key missionaries left to

[49] Thomas, "Old Memories (1975-1980)."

[50] P.M. Thomas, "Old Memories, part 11 (1984-1987)," *Himalaya Harvest* (XXXIII/2, June 2012): 14-15.

[51] Thomas, "Old Memories, part 11 (1984-1987)," 15.

[52] P.M. Thomas, "Old Memories, part 12 (1987-1990)," *Himalaya Harvest* (September 2012): 6.

[53] Harvest News, *Himalaya Harvest*, September, 2012.

[54] P.M. Thomas, "Old Memories part 12 (1987-1990)," *Himalaya Harvest* (September 2012): 7-8.

start their own ministries. Besides that about a dozen of his associates and missionaries have branched out and started their own pioneer missions. They are also now spreading to the rest of India with a few thousands of their missionaries and churches. P.G. Vargis of the Indian Evangelical Team is one of them.[55]

Today the Kashmir Evangelical Fellowship (which is now known as Himalaya Evangelical Mission) has about 475 missionaries with over 350 established churches all along the Himalayan belt right from the Tibetan border down to Burma. The Kashmir Evangelical Fellowship has spurred the founding of another six missionary organizations spread all over India with over 3000 missionaries. He handed over the leadership of the ministry in Kashmir to his son Santosh Thomas and moved to Gorakhpur, U.P., in the year 1996 and established the ministry there. Now there are 425 missionaries working in 1200 mission fields and in three regional offices. His present ministry includes training missionaries through a Missionary Training Centre, two Bible schools, Children ministry, charitable activities, leading evangelical teams, disciplining and mentoring younger leadership.[56] The ministry began by his brother-in-law C. Kunjukutty Athialy and his wife, in 1952 in Kathmandu is now growing fast from four believers at that time to several thousand believers now.[57]

Another Pentecostal move in the Himalayan region emerged through the untiring work of P.G. Vargis. Coming from a denominational background his family disinherited him for his Pentecostal faith and for his consequent decision to become a Pentecostal missionary. In 1972, resigning his military service, as a family he set out as missionary to Katra, a popular Hindu pilgrimage centre in the lower Himalayan mountains. Katra had no Christians and had never been a church in that town or in the vicinity. On reaching there, in the first gospel meeting a women who had been infested with evil spirit for twelve years was delivered through prayer. She had been treated by many which doctors but could not be

---

[55] Email from Thomas

[56] http://www.himalayamission.org/ (accessed 10/07/2014).

[57] Email from Thomas.

delivered.[58] Vargis and his wife distributed gospel tracts in different areas of the city, taught street children and visited houses to share the gospel.[59] The work among the street children, who are from outcastes, began to show some results; 24 children became part of the study programme. His wife Lily, using the Gospel of Mark taught the children alphabet, words and sentences and fed them at their home. Through this children, Vargis could get entrance to these families to share the gospel and within few months 54 people took baptism and became part of the church. In an another instance, according to his autobiography, a sister visited them for few days of prayer meetings and resulted in a revival and many miracles happened and 50 more people took baptism.[60]

Vargis and his family had to face ridicule, persecution, and even death threats. With no church or agency to financially sponsor them, they faced constant poverty and hardships. Midst of such struggles, according to Vargis, OM, Gospel Literature Service and other mission organisation sent him gospel literature free of cost.[61] Within three years the number of members had grown to 300, and daughter churches began to spring up in surrounding the mountains. Later many evangelists and lay people joined Vargis and a movement began to flow out of the church in Katra. Soon, the movement spread throughout Northern India resulted in the formation and registration of Indian Evangelical Team (IET) in 1977.[62] Vargis mentions many of the brothers and sisters who stood with him in thick and thin of the mission work and their untiring cooperate efforts had seen great results in the form of church growth and extension of the mission fields into the various states of north India.[63]

Vargis' Pentecostal and charismatic teachings has major effects on the growth of the movement. According to him, deliverance from poverty, sickness, curse, lack of peace, black magic all are included

---

[58] P.G. Vargis, *Christuvinu Vendi Himalaya Sanukkalil* (Pathankot, India: Indian Evangelical Team), 70.

[59] Vargis, *Christuvinu Vendi,* 73.

[60] Vargis, *Christuvinu Vendi,* 75-76.

[61] Vargis, *Christuvinu Vendi,* 87.

[62] Vargis, *Christuvinu Vendi,* 90.

[63] Vargis, *Christuvinu Vendi,* 92-95.

in God's salvation.[64] In his book, *The Key Miracles*, he writes, "If you believe, Jesus will help you. He is a blessing God. He is the son of David that blesses his people, their children and children's children. May be you do not have money enough to manage your home. Do you think that Jesus won't help you? His name is Merciful, Compassionate and everlasting Love. He is the God of Abraham who has promised to extend the boundary, increase the cattle, bless the fruit of the garden and bless the fruit of the womb."[65] Such a teaching of blessing and prosperity coupled with manifestations of signs and wonders have attracted many people from downtrodden background in north Indian context. Healing miracles and exorcisms delivered many from their pathetic situations. Such ministerial practices resulted in major growth in mission activities as well as church growth.

According to Vargis, IET has its presence throughout South East Asia and it has birthed more than 27 church planting movements in various regions of South East Asia. It is claimed that IET trains hundreds of Spirit-filled indigenous men and women to be effective church planters and Christian leaders through its regional Bible schools and the one accredited central leadership training centre. Today IET claims over 2300 pioneer missionaries ministering in over 6,000 Churches in Twenty States of India, and neighbouring countries of Nepal & Bhutan. One Theological College and 21 Gospel Training Centres and one orphanage have also been established. Vreeland records concerning Vargis' Indian Evangelical Team, "IET is an indigenous church planting movement established in 1972. As of March 2000, IET had ministries in 20 states in India. Currently Vargis has raised up 2,297 churches and 1,776 missionaries throughout India, Nepal and Bhutan. The growth of IET and Vargis' vision has caused him to break out as an emergent leader in Indian Pentecostalism."[66]

---

[64] P. G. Vargis, *Real Peace* (New Delhi: Faith Publishers), 45.

[65] P. G. Vargis, *The Key to Miracles* (New Delhi: Faith Publishers, 1993), 30.

[66] Derek E. Vreeland, "P. G. Vargis and the Indian Prosperity Gospel," Paper Presented in 31st Annual SPS Meeting, Lakeland, FL, USA, 16th March, 2002, 678.

Delhi and Haryana

Another important figure in the north Indian Pentecostal mission is K. V. Paul Pillai. Coming from a staunch Hindu family in Kerala, Pillai was healed by one of his Christian friends and became a Christian.[67] While he was continuing his theological education in the Hindustan Bible Institute in Madras, as team he was travelled various parts of north India for mission work. Once in Nathdwara, a temple town of Hindus, near Udaipur, the team was brutally attacked by the people around there. Pillai and friends were badly beaten by the crowd and could not get up from the ground. While lying on the ground, Pillai saw a larger crowd advancing menacingly towards them. However, another group encircled them and resisted the attackers. The attackers ultimately retreated seeing the defenders of the team and the group defended them also vanished from the scene. Then Pillai saw a strong build man standing beside him and lifted him up. As he turned to see his friends, by then the man vanished from the scene. He claims that it was the guardian angels sent by God to rescue them.[68]

Then he moved to Delhi and began to focus various people groups in the historically unreached parts of Northern India. In 1964 he established India National Inland Mission, an indigenous evangelism and church-planting ministry and travelled various parts of Uttar Pradesh and other north Indian states. In 1964, a church had established in Delhi and affiliated as Bible Church of India. By 1970, around 50 congregations were established throughout Delhi and neighbouring states.[69] In 1972, a missionary training school, Grace Bible College was established in Gurgaon, Haryana, nearby Delhi which trained hundreds of missionaries. Students from all over India as well as from Myanmar, Nepal and Bhutan are trained here.

Bethesda Children's Home is one of the humanitarian arms of India National Inland Mission, established in 1976, with the sole purpose of rescuing children that have been orphaned, abandoned or being enslaved in human trafficking or child labour camps. Moreover,

---

[67] Thomas Thonnakkal, *Dr. Paul Pillai: A Man of God with Great Vision* (Noida, India: Harvest Mission Publishers, 2002), 26-32.

[68] Thonnakkal, *Dr. Paul Pillai,* 45-46.

[69] Thonnakkal, *Dr. Paul Pillai,* 58-60.

children of convicts, who undergo jail term in Tihar Jail are also accommodated here. Since 1976, this Outreach has raised hundreds children with many of them are today in full-time Christian ministry. It is claimed that since 1964, India National Inland Mission has established hundreds of churches in India and South Asia.

Uttar Pradesh

The major cities of the state of Uttar Pradesh also witnessed coming up of Pentecostal churches and mission in these period. In 1962, an independent missionary, Maxwell George who became a Pentecostal through the ministry of George Thomas Paradeshi, came to Agra and began Pentecostal mission. He used to erect tents in different parts of the cities and preach the gospel. It is reported that he was so powerful and through his work many people joined the Pentecostal fold. Many young people committed their lives and came out for Pentecostal mission in different places of North India. Harun Masih and Motilal Isaac went to Indore, Kushwah went to Orissa, Ravi Ratan and Volish Loyal went to Jhansi and Gopal Singh went to Udaipur. Some other like Munna Singh, Harry Singh and Nihal Singh began Pentecostal mission in the city of Agra itself and also assisted Maxwell George. Subsequently, the missionaries those who were working in North India started a convention every year which was known as "All India Pentecostal Convention" and the leaders involved were Maxwell George (Agra), Christy Liddle (Dehra Doon), Celebester (Allahabad), B.R. Lenn (Mujhafar Nagar), Rana and M.K. Chacko from Delhi and Kurian Thomas from Itarsi.

Later in 1976, P.P. John from Kerala came to Agra and he belonged to the India Pentecostal Church (IPC). He began the Pentecostal mission in Agra and it is reported that hundreds of people joined Pentecostal faith. From his church many young people dedicated for the ministry and started independent Pentecostal churches in Agra. In 1977, a missionary from Tamil Nadu, Y.D. Jayaseelan came to Agra and began to preach Pentecostal faith. In 1990, he joined the Victory Church International and became the leader. Today this church has several branch churches and house churches in many of the North Indian states.

It is almost impossible to fathom all of the works by different Pentecostal missions; most of them are local and indigenous. Local missionaries work in the frontiers where many poor and downtrodden are being rescued from their wretched conditions.[70] Besides, a number of Bible colleges, orphanages and charity organisations are run by Pentecostals today, either at individual or organisational level. During 2000-2010, there was significant growth in almost all states except a few states of north India which need to be documented.

[70] See Hedlund, *Christianity is Indian,* 108-135.

Chapter 7

Conclusion

In the previous pages we have explored the history of Pentecostal movement in north India. As we have seen, it is a gigantic task to comprehend and present the history in the north encompassing all events with chronological accuracy given the vast research need to be carried out. Moreover, in many cases, the information available for the historical events and churches and organisations are sketchy and very shallow. Nevertheless, the efforts have been taken to present a true picture of the events, churches and organisations best of my knowledge and within the limitation of the availability of information.

The task of digging out the stories of the Pentecostal movement in the north is huge and unfinished. It needs life time dedication of committed pioneers just as in the case of initial Pentecostal missionaries dedicated their life for mission endeavours. Moreover, it needs financial resources and intellectual integrity to plunge into the task. Most of all, it needs a leading of the Spirit and much patient. The time has come to retrieve the Pentecostal heritage before they are lost forever. The readers, Pentecostal researchers, historians and theologians need to take up the Pentecostal movement in north India as their target of research and bring out its historical heritage to present to the future generations. Such endeavours will also help to unravel its mission history, missiology and theology. Here I encourage theological students to foray into these aspects to highlight the contribution of the movement in the larger society in emancipating the poor and the downtrodden, hence the nation building.

Before we end our discussion, it is important to draw out certain practical lessons which may be helpful:

1. Revivals can be described as the immediate reason for the formation and remarkable growth of the Pentecostal movement. They have kick-started the movement and amplified the Pentecostal church growth. As we have seen, however, revivals cannot be brought forth by human efforts or do not happen mechanically but when people of God prepare themselves and wait for the move of the Spirit, the revivals take place. Such revival move brings radical changes in the people involved in it as well as the society in which they belong to. This results in emancipation of the downtrodden people and reformation in the society.
2. The revivals may arise in various periods and places, however, it is important to translate them into church growth. One of the mistakes of early Pentecostals who received Spirit experiences was, though they involved in fervent evangelistic programmes, they were not able to translate their activities into church growth in large scale. That resulted in diminishing the thrust of the movement and later lost the power to engage in the north Indian scenario. The main reason for such a lost opportunity was the lack of strong native leadership. As we have seen, most of them were women and come from disadvantaged background without adequate financial resources as well as leadership capabilities. Even today, for a sustained growth of the Pentecostal movement in the north needs native leadership who know the culture, language and the context.
3. To sustain the growth, constant spiritual nourishment, a relevant missiology and systematic education are essential. As we have seen, the north Indian situation is unique and hard for missionaries. This entails Spirit-induced innovative missionary and pastoral methods. Organisations and churches that failed to develop such strategies have gone into oblivion. The believers are to be equipped to sustain the onslaught of social pressures as well

as to go out to witness among their fellow-beings. In other words, developing suitable local models of spirituality and missiology and biblical education are key issue.

4. The Spirit-movements require a concrete theology of its own, especially a Christology to take the movement forward, as the New Testament Epistles show us. Even though mission is growing fast and churches are being planted all over north India, the Pentecostal movement has not articulated its theology, especially justification for its unique mission practices and spiritual activities. These elements are important and vital, as they would help the movement to consolidate itself in a hostile and hard terrain of north Indian mission fields. Moreover, a strong contextual Christology relevant to the north Indian context is essential. Such a Christological articulation would assist the movement to spread the gospel message to people with different contexts and various needs. It will also help to uphold the uniqueness of Christ in the midst of religious pluralism and also disseminate the message of Christ in context of counter claims and fanatic outbursts. Otherwise, the movement may vanish into oblivion.
5. Concerted efforts are needed, rather than individualistic and self-serving mission ventures. One of the inherent handicaps often infect the Pentecostal movement is frequent splits in the movement. Personality clashes of and egos of leadership create enormous setback for the movement. Rarely do we find a schism in the name of doctrines or practices. Most of them happen due to the leadership struggle or factions created by some Pentecostal leaders. Institutions such as Bible colleges have emerged around personalities, creating factions within existing bodies as well as spinning off to form new denominations. Nevertheless, such divisions sometimes have a positive effect in the Pentecostal movement. The leaders or factions who moved away work hard to build up their mission activities that have resulted in multiplied growth which would have been rather difficult if leaders were together.

These multiplied and growing groups exhibit something of the vitality of Pentecostalism. Nevertheless, this fissiparous tendency also is counter-productive for Christian witness in a complex society seeking unity in the midst of diversity. A tendency for divisive exclusiveness on the part of some Pentecostal groups is an impediment to united witness.[1] This presupposes ecumenism among Pentecostals.

6. It is also important to include the history of Pentecostal movement in India, especially of the north as well as in the south, in the theological curriculum. The stories of movements and people that are trailblazers are to be taught to inspire future missionaries and pastors. The history of Pentecostalism is filled with colourful personalities who can be studied for lessons and models of leadership. Pastoral and mission theology should include stories of ordinary people who became great heroes and heroines of the movement.

Summing up, it is clear that what has been recorded is only a meagre part of the whole of the story. Stories of many parts of North India as well as the hard labour of the common believers are yet to be discovered and documented. This task presupposes further research, which would read 'stories from the margins'. Moreover, above-mentioned revivals and the miraculous events accompanied with them have largely contributed to the theological articulation of ordinary Pentecostals which needs to be explored and systematised. One more word is warranted: history always teaches us some lessons, however, the onus is on us to hear and correct the course of action. The History of North Indian Pentecostalism silently whispers to us to ensure that we do not forget them.

[1] Roger E. Hedlund, "Critique of Pentecostal Mission by a Friendly Evangelical," *AJPS* 8/1 (2005): 86.

Bibliography

Abraham, K. E. *Yesukristhuvinte Eliya Dassan* [*Autobiography of Pastor K.E. Abraham*], 3rd ed. Kumbanad: K. E. Abraham Foundation Publications, 2001.

Abraham, P. G. *Caste and Christianity: A Pentecostal Perspective.* Kumbhaza: Crown Books, 2003.

Abraham, Shaibu. Ordinary Indian Pentecostal Christology. Unpublished PhD Thesis, University of Birmingham, England, 2011.

Abraham, Shaibu. *Pentecostal Theology of Liberation: Holy Spirit and Holiness in the Society.* New Delhi: Christian World Imprints, 2014.

Anderson, Allan & Edmond Tang (eds.). *Asian and Pentecostal: The Charismatic Face of Christianity in Asia.* Carlisle: Regnum Books International, 2005.

Anderson, Allan. 'Revising Pentecostal History in Global Perspective.' In *Asian and Pentecostal: The Charismatic Face of Christianity in Asia.* Edited by Allan Anderson & Edmond Tang. Carlisle: Regnum Books International, 2005.

Anderson, Allan. 'Towards a Pentecostal Missiology for the Majority World.' *AJPS* 8/1 (2005): 29-47.

Anderson, Allan. *An Introduction to Pentecostalism.* Cambridge: Cambridge University Press, 2004.

Anderson, Allan. *Spreading Fires: The Missionary Nature of Early Pentecostalism.* London: SCM Press, 2007.

Anderson, Robert M. *Vision of the Disinherited: The Making of American Pentecostalism.* New York: Oxford University Press, 1979.

Barrett, David B. & Todd M. Johnson. 'Annual Statistical Table on Global Mission.' *IBMR,* 23 (January 1999): 24-25.

Barrett, David B., George T. Kurian & Todd M. Johnson (eds.). *World Christian Encyclopedia,* 2nd ed. New York: Oxford University Press, 2001.

Bergunder, Michael. 'Constructing Indian Pentecostalism: On Issues of Methodology and Presentation.' In *Asian and Pentecostal: The Charismatic Face of Christianity in Asia.* Edited by Allan Anderson & Edmond Tang. Carlisle: Regnum Books International, 2005.

Bergunder, Michael. 'Miracle Healing and Exorcism: The South Indian Pentecostal Movement in the Context of Popular Hinduism.' *International Review of Mission* XC/356, 357 (January-April 2001): 101-112.

Bergunder, Michael. 'Women and Leadership in the South Indian Pentecostal Movement.' *Dharma Deepika* 6/2 (July-December 2002): 35-40.

Bergunder, Michael. *The South Indian Pentecostal Movement in the Twentieth Century.* Cambridge: William B. Eerdmans Publishing Co., 2008.

Boyd, Robin. *An Introduction to Indian Christian Theology.* Madras: The Christian Literature Service, 1969.

Bueno, Ronald N. 'Listening to the Margins: Re-historicising Pentecostal Experiences and Identities." In *The Globalization of Pentecostalism.* Edited by M.W. Dempster, B. D. Klaus and D. Petersen. Carlisle: Regnum Books International, 1999.

Burgess, Stanley M. (ed.), *The New International Dictionary of Pentecostal and Charismatic Movements.* Michigan: Zondervan Publishing House, 2002.

Burgess, Stanley M. 'Pentecostalism in India: An Overview,' *Asian Journal of Pentecostal Studies* 4/1 (2001): 85-98.

Cerillo Jr., Agustus. 'Interpretive Approaches to the History of American Pentecostal Origins,' *Pneuma* 19/1 (Spring, 1997): 30-32.

Church of North India. http://www.cnisynod.org/beginning.aspx (accessed 8 January 2010).

Cole, Deborah Kaye. "Historiographic Approaches to Asian Pentecostalism," *AJPS* 9/1 (2006): 59-82.

David, M. D. *Missions: Cross-Cultural Encounter and Change in Western India.* Delhi: ISPCK, 2001.

Duewel, Wesley. *Revival Fire.* Michigan: Zondervan Publishing House, 1995.

Dyer, Helen S. (comp.), *Revival in India, 1905-1906.* Akola, Maharashtra: Alliance Publications, 1987.

Firth, C. B. *An Introduction to Indian Church History.* Delhi: ISPCK, 1976.

Frykenberg, Robert. E. 'Christianity in South India Since 1500: Historical Studies of Transcultural Interactions within Hindu-Muslim Environments,' *Dharma Deepika* (December 1997): 3-7.

Gabriel, Reuben Louis. 'Reflections on Indian Pentecostalism: Trends and Issues,' *Dharma Deepika,* Vol. 6, No. 2 (July-December 2002): 69-71.

Garitte, Gérard & J. N. Farquhar, *The Apostle Thomas in India according to the Acts of Thomas,* Kottayam, Kerala : [s.n.], 1972.

George, A. C. 'Pentecostal Beginnings in Travancore, South India.' *AJPS* 4/2 (2001): 215-37.

George, A. C. *Trailblazers for God: A History of the Assemblies of God of India.* Bangalore: SABC Publications, 2004.

Hedlund, Roger E. 'Critique of Pentecostal Mission by a Friendly Evangelical.' *AJPS* 8/1 (2005): 67-94.

Hedlund, Roger E. 'Indigenous Pentecostalism in India.' In *Asian and Pentecostal: The Charismatic Face of Christianity in Asia.* Edited by Allan Anderson & Edmond Tang. Carlisle: Regnum Books International, 2005.

Hedlund, Roger E. *Christianity is Indian: The Emergence of an Indigenous Community,* rev. ed. Delhi: ISPCK, 2004.

Hedlund, Roger E. *Quest for Identity: India's Churches of Indigenous Origin, The 'Little Tradition' in Indian Christianity.* Delhi: ISPCK, 2000.

Hong, Young-Gi. 'Church and Mission: A Pentecostal Perspective.' *International Review of Mission* XC/358 (July 2001): 289-308.

Hrangkhuma, F. 'Church in India.' In *Church in Asia Today: Challenges and Opportunities.* Edited by Saphir Athyal. Singapore: Asian Lausanne Committee for World Evangelism, 1996.

Hrangkhuma, F. 'Factors that Contributed to the Arrest of Mass Movements Towards Christianity in India.' In *Christianity in India: Search for Liberation and Identity.* Edited by F. Hrangkhuma. Delhi: ISPCK, 2000.

Jenkins, Philip. *The Next Christendom: The Coming of Global Christianity.* Oxford: Oxford University Press, 2002.

Jeyakumar, D. Arthur. 'Group Conversion Movements to Christianity in the Indian Sub-Continent,' *Indian Church History Review* XXXIX/2 (December 2005): 63-73.

Jeyakumar, D. Arthur. *History of Christianity in India: Selected Themes.* Delhi: ISPCK, 2004.

Jones, W. W. 'Mass Movement as Missionary Dream and Reality,' *Indian Church History Review* XXVIII/2 (1994): 135-151.

Joy, K. T. *The Mar Thoma Church: A Study of its Growth and Contribution.* Kottayam, Kerala: Good Shepherd Press, 1986.

Kochukunju, Muthapackal. "Malankara Kanda Maha Unarv" (Malayalam) (The Great Revival that Saw Malankara) *Maranatha Voice.* October 10, 2006, 8-9 and 14.

Lindner, John. *The Mountain Shall Sing: The Story of P.M. Thomas and Himalaya Evangelical Mission.* Gorakhpur: Himalaya Evangelical Mission, 2003.

Lord, Andrew M. The Holy Spirit and Contextualization, *AJPS* 4/2 (2001): 201-213.

Lukose, Wessly. 'A Contextual Missiology of the Spirit: A Study of Pentecostalism in Rajasthan, India.' Unpublished PhD Thesis, University of Birmingham, England, 2009.

Lukose, Wessly. 'Pentecostal Beginnings in Rajasthan: Part One,' *AJPS* 12:2 (2009): 231-256.

Ma, Wonsuk. 'Asian (Classical) Pentecostalism: Theology in Context.' *Dharma Deepika* 6/2 (July-December 2002): 13-33.

Ma, Wonsuk. 'Asian Pentecostalism: A Religion whose only Limit is the Sky.' *Journal of Beliefs & Values* 25/2 (August 2004): 191-204.

Martin, Paul C. 'The Ceylon Pentecostal Mission,' in *Christianity is Indian: The Emergence of an Indigenous Community*, rev. ed. Edited by Roger E. Hedlund. Delhi: ISPCK, 2004.

Massey, James. 'Christianity among the Dalits in North India with Special Reference to Punjab.' In *Christianity in India: Search for Liberation and Identity.* Edited by F. Hrangkhuma. Delhi: ISPCK, 2000.

Massey, James. 'Christians in North India: Historical Perspective with Special Reference to Christians in Panjab.' *Religion and Society* XXXIV/3 (September 1987): 88-106.

Mathew, Saju. *Kerala Penthecosthu Charithram,* 2nd ed. Bilaspur: Margam Books, 2006.

McGee, Gary B. & S. M. Burgess, 'India.' *The New International Dictionary of Pentecostal and Charismatic Movements.* Michigan: Zondervan Publishing House, 2002: 118-126.

McGee, Gary B. '"Latter Rain" Falling in the East: Early-Twentieth-Century Pentecostalism in India and the Debate over Speaking in Tongues.' *Church History* 68/3 (1999): 648-665.

McGee, Gary B. 'Pentecostal and Pentecostal-like Movements (1860-1910).' *NIDPCM*. Michigan: Zondervan, 2002, 118-119.

McGee, Gary B. "Pentecostal Phenomena and Revivals in India: Implications for Indigenous Church Leadership." *International Bulletin of Missionary Research* 20/3 (July 1996): 112-117.

McGee, Gary B. 'The Calcutta Revival of 1907 and the Reformulation of Charles Parham's Bible Evidence Doctrine.' *AJPS* 6/1 (2003): 123-143.

Miller, Basil, *Praying Hide: A Man of Prayer.* Michigan: Zondervan Publishing House, 1943.

Miller, Donald E. and Tetsunao Yamamori, *Global Pentecostalism: The New Face of Christian Social Engagement.* Berkeley, California: University of California Press, 2007.

Moffett, Samuel Hugh. *A History of Christianity in Asia: 1500-1900, Vol. II.* New York: Orbis Books, 2005.

Moffett, Samuel Hugh. *A History of Christianity in Asia: Beginnings to 1500, Vol.1.* 2nd rev. ed. New York: Orbis Books, 1998.

Mundadan, A. Mathias. 'The Changing Task of Christian History.' In *Enlarging the Story: Perspectives on Writing World Christian History.* Edited by Wilbert R. Shenk. Maryknoll, NY: Orbis Books, 2002.

Mundadan, A. Mathias. *History of Christianity in India, Vol. I: From the Beginning up to the Middle of the Sixteenth Century (up to 1542).* Bangalore: Church History Association of India, 1989.

Neumann, Mikel. *Home Groups for Urban Cultures.* Pasadena, California: William Carey Library, 1999.

New Life Assembly of God, Chennai. http://www.nlag.org.in/about_us.htm (accessed 22 December 2009).

Orr, J. Edwin. *Evangelical Awakenings in Southern Asia.* Minneapolis: Bethany Fellowship, 1975.

Orr, J. Edwin. The Outpouring of the Spirit in Revival and Awakening and its Issue in Church Growth (British Church Growth Association, 2000). http://www.churchmodel.org.uk/Orr% 20HS%20BOOKLET%20A4. pdf (accessed 12 January 2010).

Parmar, S. L. 'The Church in North India,' *Ecumenical Review* XX/1 (January 1968): 72-83.

Perayil, Varghese. *The Oath of Coonan Cross.* Adoor, Kerala: Kerala Study Centre, 2007.

Philip, E. M. *The Indian Christians of St. Thomas.* 1950.

Philip, Finny. 'The Thomas Mathews Revolution.' *Cross and Crown* 36/1 (November 2005 - March 2006): 18-23.

Philip, Glory M. 'Celestial Celebration of Saints: Navapur `07.' *Cross & Crown* 37/2 (November-December 2007): 11-16.

Philipose, A. *The Apostolic Origin and Early History of the Syrian Church of Malabar.* London: The Christian Literature Society, 1904.

Pickett, J. Waskom. *Christian Mass Movements in India.* New York: Abingdon Press, 1933.

Ponraj, S. Devasahayam. *From Graveyard to Vineyard: Transformation in Bihar (The Historical Development, 1790-2008).*

Prakash, P. Surya 'Contribution of Sadhu Sundhar Singh to the Indigenous Christian Movement in India,' *Christianity is Indian: The Emergence of an Indigenous Community,* rev. ed. Edited by Roger E. Hedlund. Delhi: ISPCK, 2004.

Pulikottil, Paulson. 'Emergence of Indian Pentecostalism.' *Dharma Deepika* 6/2 (July-December 2002): 47-58.

Pulikottil, Paulson. 'Ramankutty Paul: A Dalit Contribution to Pentecostalism.' In *Asian and Pentecostal: The Charismatic Face of Christianity in Asia.* Edited by Allan Anderson and Edmond Tang. Carlisle: Regnum Books International, 2005.

Pulikottil, Paulson. "As East and West Met in God's Own Country: Encounter of Western Pentecostalism with Native Pentecostalism in Kerala," *AJPS* 5/1 (2002): 5-22.

Raj, S. Albones. 'Mass Religious Conversion as Protest Movement: A Framework,' *Religion and Society* XXVIII/4 (1981): 58-66.

Samuel Kutty, T. S. *The Place and Contribution of Dalits in Select Pentecostal Churches in Central Kerala from 1922-1972.* Delhi: ISPCK, 2000.

Samuel, P. S. *Christhuvil Oru Samarppitha Jeevitham: An Autobiography.* Raipur: The Church of God, Raipur, 2006, 29-30.

Satyavrata, Ivan M. "Contextual Perspectives on Pentecostalism as a Global Culture: A South Asian View,' in *The Globalization of Pentecostalism*, edited by M. W. Dempster, B. D. Klaus and D. Petersen. Carlisle: Regnum Books International, 1999.

Shenk, Wilbert R. (ed.), *Enlarging the Story: Perspectives on Writing World Christian History*. Maryknoll, NY: Orbis Books, 2002.

Simmons, Roger. *Vision, Mission and a Movement.* Udaipur, Rajasthan: Native Missionary Movement, 2008.

Snaitang, O. L. 'The Indigenous Pentecostal Movement in Northeast India.' *Dharma Deepika* 6/2 (July-December, 2002): 5-11.

Sumithra, Sunand. *Christian Theologies from an Indian Perspective.* Bangalore: Theological Book Trust, 1995.

Tangelder, Johan D. Azusa Street & Beyond: 100 Years of Commentary on the Global Pentecostal/Charismatic Movement, edited by Grant McClung. Gainesville, Florida: Bridges-Logos, 2006.

Thekkedath, Joseph. *History of Christianity in India, Vol. II, From the Middle of the Sixteenth Century to the Seventeenth Century.* Bangalore: Theological Publications in India, 1982.

Thomas, Kurien. *God's Trailblazer in India and Around the World.* Itarsi: Kurien Thomas, 1986.

Thomas, P. *Christians and Christianity in India and Pakistan.* London: George Allen & Unwin, 1954.

Thomas, P. M. "Old Memories (1975-1980)," *Himalaya Harvest* (XXXII/4 December 2011).

Thomas, P. M. "Old Memories, part 11 (1984-1987)," *Himalaya Harvest* (XXXIII/2, June 2012): 8-17.

Thomas, P. M. "Old Memories, part 12 (1987-1990)," *Himalaya Harvest* (September 2012): 6-14.

Thomas, V. V. 'Pentecostalism among the Dalits in Kerala from 1909 to the Present: A Subaltern Reading.' *UBS Journal* 3/2 (September 2005): 89-94.

Thompson, Paul. *The Voice of the Past: Oral History* 2nd ed. New York: Oxford University Press, 1988.

Thonnakkal, Thomas. *Dr. Paul Pillai: A Man of God with Great Vision.* Noida: Harvest Mission Publishers, 2002.

Varghese, V. Titus & P. P. Philip, *Glimpses of the History of the Christian Churches in India.* Madras: The Christian Literature Society, 1983.

Vargis, P. G. *Christuvinuvendi Himalaya Sanukkalil.* Pathankot, India: Indian Evangelical Team.

Webster, John C. B. *The Christian Community and Change in Nineteenth Century North India.* Delhi: Macmillan, 1976.

Wilson, Everett A. 'They Crossed the Red Sea, Didn't They?: Critical History and Pentecostal Beginning' in *The Globalization of Pentecostalism*, edited by M. W. Dempster, B. D. Klaus, D. Petersen. Carlisle: Regnum Books International, 1999.

Index

I

J

K

L

M

N

O

P

R